PRACTICAL SOCIAL WORK

Series Editor: Jo Campling

(BASW)

Social work is at an important stage in its development. All professions must be responsive to changing social and economic conditions if they are to meet the needs of those they serve. This series focuses on sound practice and the specific contribution which social workers can make to the well-being of our society.

The British Association of Social Workers has always been conscious of its role in setting guidelines for practice and in seeking to raise professional standards. The conception of the Practical Social Work series arose from a survey of BASW members to discover where they, the practitioners in social work, felt there was the most need for new literature. The response was overwhelming and enthusiastic, and the result is a carefully planned, coherent series of books. The emphasis is firmly on practice, set in a theoretical framework. The books will inform, stimulate and promote discussion, thus adding to the further development of skills and high professional standards. All the authors are practitioners and teachers of social work representing a wide variety of experience.

Jo Campling

PRACTICAL SOCIAL WORK

Series Editor: Jo Campling

BASW

Working with Abused Children

Celia Doyle

MACMILLAN

First published 1990

Published by
MACMILLAN EDUCATION LTD
Houndmills, Basingstoke, Hampshire RG21 2XS
and London
Companies and representatives
throughout the world

Printed in Hong Kong

British Library Cataloguing in Publication Data
Doyle, Celia, *1950–*
Working with Abused Children
1. Children. Abuse by adults
I. Title
362.7′044
ISBN 0–333–48036–8 (hardcover)
ISBN 0–333–48037–6 (paperback)

Series Standing Order
If you would like to receive future titles in this series as they are
published, you can make use of our standing order facility. To place a
standing order please contact your bookseller or, in case of difficulty,
write to us at the address below with your name and address and the
name of the series. Please state with which title you wish to begin your
standing order. (If you live outside the United Kingdom we may not
have the rights for your area, in which case we will forward your order
to the publisher concerned.)

Customer Services Department, Macmillan Distribution Ltd,
Houndmills, Basingstoke, Hampshire, RG21 2XS, England.

For my children

Contents

Acknowledgements

A debt of gratitude is owed to Dr Margaret Oates, who first awakened, then sustained, my interest in the subject of child abuse and to David N. Jones, who has given me constant support and encouragement over the years. Thanks are also due to all those colleagues who have been a source of inspiration including Dr Peter Barbor, Carl Blakey, Madeleine Collinge, Judy Fawcett, Tom Narducci, Andy Perrins and Jenny Still. I am also grateful to Jean Moore, whose training opened up new horizons.

The contributions of Marie, Helen and Sarah are much appreciated. The book is all the richer for the assistance with reading material and references provided so ably and for so many years by Christine Smakowska, NSPCC librarian and her colleagues. I am especially grateful to my mother, Joan Doyle, who read through the drafts and advised on style and grammar.

On the domestic front sincere thanks are due to Sue Buckley, whose calmness and care of the babies proved indispensable, to our eldest son Alexander for his help and, above all, to my husband John for his unstinting practical and moral support

CELIA DOYLE

Introduction

The inspiration for this book comes from the life and death of a small boy, Darryn Clarke. He was killed by his mother's partner and was the subject of a public enquiry (Clarke, 1979). Shortly after his death, as a participant in a child abuse training course, I was asked to present the report as though I were Darryn himself giving evidence to the inquiry. For the first time I saw the events through the eyes of the abused child.

This caused a profound change in the focus of my work. Previously I had concentrated on helping the parents. It was, after all, easier to communicate with fellow adults. Furthermore I could largely dismiss the pain felt by the children if I concentrated on the parents' needs. Their distress was considerable but not as poignant as that of their young offspring. But, having relived Darryn's last weeks, I could no longer ignore the plight of the abused child.

From then on I tried to look at abuse from the children's perspective. I sought ways to communicate with all youngsters from the smallest infant to the most sophisticated and cynical of adolescents. I slowly began to understand how best we might give them real and lasting help. This book is the product of those years of striving to focus on the abused child.

Modern day concern for the welfare of children can trace its origins back to late nineteenth-century philanthropy. The emphasis was on rescuing the child and punishing their parents. Nigel Parton in his historical perspective on child abuse writes, 'Families were expected to take full responsibility for their members and if this was not possible the state would intervene in a harsh, controlling way' (Parton, 1985, p. 36).

The earlier twentieth century saw a gradual change in attitude; the state was seen to have some responsibility for the welfare of its citizens including the youngest. State support for 'poor but honest' parents became an additional ingredient although rescue of neglected or mistreated children remained the main method of intervention.

The evacuation of children during the Second World War brought home to a much larger and more influential section of society the widespread nature of child neglect and deprivation. It was recognised that rescue and punishment was no longer a feasible means of managing the problem. In addition the death of Dennis O'Neill (1945) at the hands of his foster father demonstrated that removal was not always the answer. Therefore for the majority of cases reform of the parents was seen to be more appropriate.

In recent times the main aim of intervention in child abuse cases has been to 're-form' abusive families or, in the most serious and intractable cases, to rescue the child and punish the parents. However, as described and illustrated in the first two chapters children are emotionally imprisoned by abusive experiences. Even after removal from home or reformation of their family's functioning they may not be truly 'rescued' because they can still carry a burden of confusing, conflicting, emotions. They are often left to cope with negative feelings towards themselves and, paradoxically, positive feelings towards the perpetrators.

The emphasis of the following three chapters is on releasing the children from the morass of potentially destructive emotions which ensnare them in an unhappy situation, however caring the nature of their new substitute home or their 'reformed' original families. These chapters examine individual, family and group work which can be undertaken by professionals, especially those with only modest training or experience and constrained by limits on time, space or facilities. These chapters are designed to offer practical guidance and encouragement to a wide variety of workers and are not confined to 'experts' in specialised settings. The suggestions have all been tried, tested and found to be helpful by myself and by colleagues, including those in local authority settings.

Substitute care with all its problems and benefits is examined. The last two chapters discuss prevention and ways of releasing adults who are still imprisoned by their childhood experiences. Many new initiatives in these two areas are springing up. Perhaps the early twenty-first century will see the dawning of a new age in child welfare – away from simple rescue/removal and punishment, away even from reform – to prevention and, for those cases where this fails, to intervention which ensures the complete release of all the victims.

The term 'child abuse' refers in this book to the physical or emotional mistreatment and neglect of children or their sexual exploitation, in circumstances for which the parents can be held responsible through acts of commission or omission. The word 'parent' includes natural, adoptive, step and foster parents. 'Child' refers to youngsters from birth to eighteen years. The term 'abused child' will often be used not only to mean the primary victim; children who are often called 'non-abused' siblings are here considered to be secondary victims if they have witnessed the mistreatment of their brothers or sisters.

All family members are important and all can suffer in cases of child abuse. Parents in particular must always be treated with respect and sensitivity. However there is a need to concentrate on understanding the victims of abuse and determining the best possible help for them. A significant proportion of the public inquiries, which have followed the deaths of children, have highlighted the fact that some social workers have become so preoccupied with the needs of the parents that they have overlooked those of the children to the detriment of everyone involved. In this book all identifying information and names in case material have been altered unless the case has been the subject of a public inquiry. This is indicated by the publication year of the inquiry report appearing after the child's name. The references for these documents can be found in the list of inquiry reports which is separate from the main bibliography.

Finally, much of this book is concerned with practical ways of helping children. Some of the ideas are drawn from other areas of social work such as bereavement counselling and work with handicapped children. Conversely, many of the models and methods of intervention suggested here may be useful for practitioners working with client groups other than abused children.

1
The Perspective of the Abused Child

Some children who are abused are only too happy to be rescued from their homes. Some may continually complain about their mistreatment and eventually settle happily with substitute carers. Many other youngsters, even those who have been seriously abused, defend their parents, hide their injuries, guard the family secret and try to avoid removal from home. This chapter attempts to look at the abuse from the child's perspective and in doing so throw some light on the apparent paradox of the victim who resists 'rescue'.

The child as a family member

The family is an important unit in most societies. It has played a significant role in politics and in the exchange of property. Generally, children from a variety of cultures are brought up to have a healthy respect for their families. For example, the Judeo-Christian tradition emphasises the theme encompassed by the injunction, 'Honour thy father and thy mother'.

'Blood is thicker than water'

There is a strong belief in the blood-tie. 'Blood is thicker than water' is a familiar saying. Before the comparatively recent introduction, mainly in developed countries, of forms of social security benefits, weaker family members relied on the stronger ones for sustenance. In many poorer countries even today ageing parents depend on their offspring for material support. The older generation therefore has a vested interest in emphasising the importance of loyalty to family members and the obligation owed to blood relatives.

One way of reinforcing messages to children is through folk-tales

1

and nursery rhymes. A study of fairy stories world-wide shows that where a child is mistreated it is generally at the hands of a non-family member or a step-parent. Cinderella and Snow White are examples from favourite Western tales. Nursery rhymes often describe a child who is beaten but who apparently deserves punishment as 'Jack and Jill' and 'Little Polly Flinders'. Occasionally in fairy-tales parents are partially responsible for their children's suffering but are unable to help in any other way. One example is the version of Hansel and Gretel in which the poverty-stricken parents leave the children in the wood because they cannot bear to see them starve to death. Children learn that they may be mistreated by people who are not really part of their family, but if they suffer at the hands of their parents it is either because they deserve punishment or because the parent is acting in their best interests.

There are implications in this for the adopted, fostered or step-child. Despite the fact that in these relationships the blood-tie is not present, the belief in its strength is significant. Children who have lost a natural parent may well feel that they have been abandoned by the person to whom they belong by virtue of the blood-tie. They may feel unable to take the care of substitute parents for granted. They believe that they must be especially good in order to guard against being abandoned again. Many boys and girls who have lost a parent feel that they were in some way responsible for the parent's departure. If their new carer mistreats them, they may assume it is because they are unlovable. They have caused their natural parent to leave and the second parent to reject them. There is therefore no escape from the abuse because in their own eyes they are unattractive to any carer.

'Like father, like son'

Associated with the blood-tie is the widely held belief in inherited tendencies. Familiar phrases such as 'like father, like son' and 'a chip off the old block' reflect this belief. Children do not want to think of their parent as weak, cruel or evil because these characteristics reflect on the children themselves. Jocelyn Peters referring to children with a range of family difficulties writes, 'In a close-knit family community, distress and deprivation will draw the members more tightly together. Disapproval of a parent means to a child disapproval of himself' (Peters, 1966 p. 74).

Playground talk often consists of boys and girls boasting that their father or mother is stronger, braver or cleverer than those of their school mates. Children bathe in their parent's reflected glory so they have a vested interest in interpreting their parent's cruel behaviour as a display of strength. This desire to be the child of someone virtuous is again reflected in, and reinforced by, those fairy-tales that tell of a good child of apparently poor or wicked parents turning out to be, in reality, the offspring of rich or benign ones.

One victim of abuse called Sarah came to dislike her father early in childhood. She recognised that this was, in her own words, 'a big decision for a child'. Echoing the words of Jocelyn Peters, Sarah's disapproval of her father led, inevitably, to self-disapproval. This resulted in a loss of self-esteem which meant that she submitted to both physical and sexual abuse because she felt she had no right to resist.

Attachment behaviour

Bonding and attachment are important features associated with family life. Bonding usually refers to the process from parent to child that starts in pregnancy and reaches a peak in the first hours and days after birth. It is argued that successful bonding helps parents respond positively to their new infant and meet the very many demands that the baby makes. This is a controversial theory but it has influenced maternity services to the extent that in many countries separation between parents and infant after birth is now avoided wherever possible.

Attachment refers to the reciprocal relationship between parent and child in the early years especially during the first year. Psychiatrist John Bowlby (1953) identified the need of infants for a strong attachment to a caregiver. The primary caregiver for a baby is his or her mother. Infants of only a few days old prefer their mother's face to other faces (Carpenter, 1974), their mother's voice to other voices (Mills and Melhuish, 1974) and can distinguish their own mother's milk from that of other women (MacFarlane, 1977). It would therefore seem possible for a child to develop a strong attachment to a parent despite the fact that bonding and attachment from the parent to child is weak. This will be particularly true of those cases where parents, although sometimes abusing their children, try hard to care for them.

Sometimes abuse of a child does not start until the youngster has developed an attachment to the parents. Furthermore a strong bond can be formed with the non-abusing parent. Children may not want to leave home or upset the family because of the love they feel for the non-abusing parent.

The natural world has provided for small animals to be looked after by substitutes in the absence of their own parents. If small animals could not form attachments to any other than their biological mother they would face certain death if she cannot look after them. Similarly children can become attached to alternative caregivers.

> The child's willingness to redirect his attachment behaviour away from an inadequate parent is indicative of the pressing need felt by the child for an attachment of some description. It is difficult to over-estimate the importance of that need. If attachment is successful, the child has an opportunity to become secure in his exploration of the physical and emotional aspects of his development. (Bolton, 1983)

This ability to redirect attachment behaviour is the basis of successful adoptions and step-parenting. However it again means that the child may attach to a foster, step or adoptive parent who has little affection for the girl or boy in question. Youngsters whose attempts to be cared for by their natural parent have failed will be all the more desperate to cling to the substitute caregivers, providing that they have given up all hope of being nurtured by their natural parents.

Some abused children live in such isolated families that there seems to be no alternative to the inadequate parent. They cannot redirect their attachment behaviour because a substitute is not available. They have little option but to continue to focus all their energies on trying to attract the abusive parent.

The child as a victim

Hostages, kidnap victims and concentration camp prisoners can, despite their suffering, demonstrate loyalty and affection towards their persecutors. An examination of the circumstances in which this may occur will provide some understanding of why many mistreated children show such a strong attachment to their abusing parents.

Hostages and kidnap victims

In hostage situations (which here include kidnaps) negotiators recognise that victims frequently develop positive feelings towards their captors and show hostility towards any rescuers. 'Even in the face of an armed officer of the law, the victim would offer himself as a human shield for his abductor. As absurd as this may seem, such behaviour had been observed by law enforcement officers throughout the world' (Strenz, 1980, p. 147).

This paradoxical phenomenon has been termed the 'Stockholm syndrome'. Its name derives from the events in Sweden in August 1973 when four employees of the Svergis Kredit Bank were held hostage for 131 hours by Jan-Erik Olsson and Clark Olofsson. It became clear that during the seige the hostages, despite being law-abiding citizens, were more afraid of the police than they were of their captors. The bank employees defended the robbers and showed no hatred towards them. One fell in love with a robber and expressed the wish to marry him.

There appear to be a number of psychological factors which enable a victim to cope with the stress of the situation and which may lead to the Stockholm syndrome. First there is denial. It is more reassuring to believe that the captors intend no harm, than to recognise that they may well be prepared to maim and kill. One hostage of the hijack of TWA flight 355 in 1976 expressed the belief that the bombs held by the hijackers were fakes even after one of the bombs had killed or injured four bomb disposal officers.

At a time of disaster and terror in which there is some possibility of escape, individuals may panic, scream and run. However, in most hostage situations the captors ensure that the victims are trapped with no means of exit. This results in what Martin Symonds has termed 'frozen fright':

> This superficiality appears to be a cooperative and friendly behaviour that confuses even the victim, the criminal, the family and friends of the victim, the police and society in general . . . the victims narrowly focus all their energy on survival, exclusively concentrating on the terrorist. This reaction is enhanced by the criminal terrorist's intent to totally dominate the victim. The terrorist creates a hostile environment and thwarts any efforts that would reduce this domination. The victim then feels isolated from others, powerless and helpless. (Symonds, 1980, pp. 131–2).

All this is reminiscent of the frozen watchfulness of the battered infant and the feelings of helplessness and isolation recounted by many victims of child abuse.

Fear and anger may be repressed or turned, not against the captor because in the hostages' impotent state that would be too uncomfortable, but against the rescuing authorities. There is a sense in which both captors and captives feel united against the outside world. The threat within is transferred to an external menace. This does not disappear as soon as rescue is achieved victims; of the Stockholm syndrome may

> remain hostile toward the police after the siege has ended. The 'original' victims in Stockholm still visit their abductors, and one former hostage is engaged to Olofsson. South American victims visit their former captors in

jail. Others have begun defense funds for them. A hostile hostage is the price that law enforcement must pay for a living hostage. (Strenz, 1980, p. 149)

Free from anger and fear of their captors and with their focus on those holding them at their mercy, the victims will search for evidence to confirm their hope that the captors are really acting in their interests. Acts, such as the captors arranging for the provision of food or allowing the victim to make himself more comfortable, are seen by the captive as proof of the hostage-takers' kindness and concern for his welfare. Hostages and abused children have in common the fact that, although they are in the power of someone who may threaten their safety, they cling to him because they are dependant on the captor/abusing parent to provide life's necessities.

There is furthermore a sense in which the hostages feel that they owe their lives to their captors. Charles Bahn explains that in the case of hostage situations:

> we have something that goes beyond mere terror and is a highly credible threat to life; once that happens, from the moment that it's not carried out, we have the beginning of the gratitude that builds up on the return of one's life from the individual who made a credible threat and nevertheless is not acting upon it. (Bahn, 1089, p. 152)

For the abused child there may be a mounting feeling of gratitude towards the abusing parent because children, particularly abused children, believe that their parents could kill them. Dorothy Bloch after years of working with children and studying their fears and fantasies concluded:

> Children are universally disposed to the fear of infanticide by both their physical and their physiological stage of development and the intensity of that fear depends on the incidence of traumatic events and on the degree of violence and of love they have experienced. . . . Why shouldn't children be afraid of being killed? To begin with consider their size. Is there anyone more killable? (Bloch, 1979, p. 3)

Concentration camp prisoners

There are a number of similarities between the victims of hostage situations, concentration camp prisoners and abused children. All are innocent, unsuspecting victims imprisoned and mistreated emotionally and/or physically by aggressors who feel that they have to hold the balance of power and have to be in total control of the victims.

Sarah Davidson, an Israeli housewife, was on the Air France airbus flight 139 which was hijacked and flown to Entebbe, Uganda in 1976. She kept a diary and in it noted how upset she was by the way her fellow passengers would agree with the suggestions of a hijacker called Bose, clapping every time he made a speech. Reflecting on what was happening she wrote:

All these years I could not comprehend the holocaust. Year in, year out, I read what is written on the subject, and I see the films and hear the horrifying testimonies, and I don't understand. Why did the Jews enter the gas chambers so quietly? Why did they go like sheep to the slaughter when they had nothing to lose? I needed the nightmare at Entebbe to comprehend. . . . The German man adopted a pleasant manner. He was a concealed enemy, pretending, tempting his victims to believe his good intentions. . . . If he had said to march in a certain direction where his colleagues were awaiting us with machine guns, ready to mow us down, we would have gone. (Dobson and Payne, 1977, pp. 226–7)

The child psychiatrist Bruno Bettleheim who was himself a concentration camp victim observed how the prisoners went through stages of adaptation. Firstly they would regress to the state of a dependant child; this was partly induced by camp rules such as those which resulted in prisoners soiling themselves. The prisoners became increasingly compliant as they realised how dependant they were on the goodwill of the guards. Eventually many prisoners went beyond compliance and began to accept the values of the guards. Some long-standing prisoners took pride in copying the verbal and physical aggression of the guards towards fellow prisoners and would try to make SS uniforms for themselves (Bettleheim, 1979).

Another study of adaptive behaviour in the camps noted that after the initial response of shock and terror apathy set in, this 'was often psychologically protective and may be thought of as providing a kind of transitional emotional hibernation' (Chodoff, 1981, p. 4). It is this apathy which can also overtake some abused children so that they no longer look for any escape and simply accept their mistreatment. The same author notes that:

Regressive behaviour of a greater or lesser degree was almost universal, being induced in the prisoners by the overwhelming infantilizing pressures to which they were subjected and by the need to stifle aggressive impulses . . . . It appears that the most important personality defenses among concentration camp inmates were denial and isolation of affect. Some form of companionship with others was indispensable, since a completely isolated individual could not have survived in the camps, but the depth of such companionship was usually limited by the overpowering egotistical demands of self-preservation. (Chodoff, 1981, p. 4)

This is an echo of the isolation felt by child abuse victims. The relationship problems caused by the need for self-preservation is illustrated in the next chapter by one abused child, Sarah, in relation to her sister.

It seems that the identification with the camp guards described by Bettleheim is an example of the basic human need to see goodness associated with power. Prisoners may believe they will survive if their guards are underneath the surface kind, just and interested in their welfare. The prisoners will therefore attach great importance to any slight gesture of kindness. Solzhenitsyn describes one experience he had as a Russian concentration camp prisoner

> in the morning the Gaoler came in without the Duty Officer and greeted them quite humanely, no, it was even more precious than that 'Good morning' . . . grateful for the warmth of the voice and the warmth of that dishwater, they drifted off to sleep until noon. (Solzhenitsyn, 1974)

As in the case of hostages, camp prisoners can feel grateful if their lives are spared. Solzhenitsyn describes how a fellow prisoner

> was taken twice into the forest at night for a supposed execution. The firing squad levelled its rifles at him and then they dropped them and he was taken back to prison . . . he is alive and healthy and does not even cherish a grudge about this. (Solzhenitsyn, 1974, p. 448)

When adults can react with such a lack of resentment it is less surprising that children should feel grateful and forgiving towards parents who, although seeming to threaten their lives, do not (in most cases) actually kill them.

In *The Gulag Archipelago* Solzhenitsyn lists the various tortures used to weaken the resistance of prisoners. Many of these are reminiscent of the behaviour of abusing parents. Psychological methods include the use of night-time when the victim lacks his daytime equanimity and common sense. Marie, a victim of abuse, described being pulled out of bed at one o'clock in the morning to be interrogated by her father about his uncleaned shoes. Foul language and humiliation are often used; these were very much part of Sarah's account of her father's behaviour described in the next chapter.

'Psychological contrast' was the term used by Solzhenitsyn to describe the 'good guy, bad guy' tactics used in many interrogation situations and by hostage-takers.

> for a whole or part of the interrogation period, the interrogator would be extremely friendly. . . . Suddenly he would brandish a paperweight and

shout 'Foo, you rat! I'll put nine grams of lead in your skull! . . .' or as a variation on this: two interrogators would take turns. One would shout and bully, the others would be friendly, almost gentle. (Solzhenitsyn, 1974 p. 104).

This is reminiscent of the parents of abused children. The abuser may be violent, threatening or coldly callous one moment and then, perhaps feeling remorseful, be loving and tender the next; alternatively one parent may be persistently cruel whereas the other parent is kind and caring.

Persuasion, inducing confusion, intimidation accompanied by enticement and promises and 'playing on one's affection for those one loved' were other psychological methods of torture cited by Solzhenitsyn. Physical methods included: burning with cigarettes (such burns are also a sign of child abuse), tickling, beating, locking in a bed-bug infested room, not allowing victims to sleep and forcing them to stand or kneel for long periods. All such methods are familiar in the field of child abuse. It is therefore hardly surprising that mistreated children, like prisoners subjected to torture, will become compliant and offer little resistance to the demands of their abusers.

The roots of resistance

Many, but not all, victims of hostage situations, concentration camps or child abuse show compliant behaviour or respond positively to their aggressors. Those that show some resistance often have a strong value system or an alternative model of behaviour to which they cling tenaciously. Solzhenitsyn himself condemned the treatment to which he was subjected. Chodoff in his study of holocaust survivors noted that certain political and religious groups were exceptions to the general response of denial and isolation (Chodoff, 1981, p. 4) and Strenz cites ambassador Geoffrey Jackson and Dr Claude Fly as examples of men who retained an aura of aloofness and did not exhibit the Stockholm syndrome. Similarly children who are subjected to mistreatment at the hands of a newly arrived step-parent or who have by other means lived for a while in a non-abusing family may well resist and complain because they know there are alternative forms of parental behaviour.

Strenz noted that the Stockholm syndrome is likely to be absent when captors showed no kindness towards their victims:

> Those victims who had negative contacts with the subjects did not evidence concern for them . . . some of these victims had been physically abused by the subjects. They obviously did not like their abuse and advocated the maximum penalty be imposed. (Strenz, 1980, p. 143)

It seems that if children live with two constantly abusing parents they will not have the same sense of loyalty and concern for the parents. The same is true if one parent is actively abusive and the other indifferent to the children's plight. Dorothy Bloch noted, 'In no case did the child feel loved by either parent . . . with these children the abusive and hating parent seems to be unworthy of respect and in some instances "didn't deserve to live", and the other parent seemed at best, passive and neutral' (Bloch, 1979, p. 237).

The victim as a child

Many hostage, kidnap and concentration camp victims are adults who, despite the process of regression, have experiences of life from which they can draw strength plus a fully developed intellect which they can use to rationalise their experiences. Abused children do not have these advantages. They are imprisoned by overwhelming emotions and, in cases of longstanding abuse, by an abnormal learning process.

The impact of emotions

There are many emotions which lead abused children to believe that they are in the wrong and the abusing adults in the right. It is interesting to note how the key emotions mirror the developmental process identified by Professor Erik Erikson. He argued that the healthy person progresses through eight positive stages which result in the establishment of a sense of basic trust, autonomy, initiative, industry, identity, intimacy, generativity and ego integrity. The alternative progression results in the acquisition of the sense of – basic mistrust, shame/doubt, guilt, inferiority, role confusion, isolation, stagnation and despair (Erikson, 1965, pp. 239–61).

Fear and mistrust – these feelings are closely related. Abused children are unable to trust those who are meant to be protecting and caring for them. In their state of mistrust and uncertainty they are beset by a number of fears. In some cases the fear is quite straightforward. One child will not talk about the parent's violence for fear of future beatings. Another may have been threatened. Sexual abusers are particularly adept at playing on a child's fears in order to secure his or her silence. Often children are not so much afraid for themselves as for their loved ones. One victim, Marie, kept quiet about her father's behaviour because she was worried about what would happen to her mother and siblings if she was removed from the family. Some children feel impelled to submit to abuse without resistance in the hope that this will keep their younger brothers and sisters safe.

Fear of alternatives is another common and understandable fear. Young children assume that if their parent mistreats them it is because every parent behaves in that way. Sarah, in Chapter 2, believed that all headmasters and fathers beat the children in their care. She would have resisted any attempt to place her with foster parents because in her inexperienced eyes they would probably have been as bad if not worse than her father; she had a 'better the devil you know' philosophy. Many abusive families and abused children are isolated with little opportunity of observing alternative family models. Mistreated children, lacking basic trust may well take a long time before they can accept that other adults are well-intentioned.

Fear of being killed is a more complex concept. Dorothy Bloch, as noted in the previous section, concluded from her clinical experience that children fear they may be killed by their parents. Although Freud dwelt at length on the later part of the story of Oedipus, which covers his murdering his father to marry his mother, he did not mention the first part which tells of the attempts of the parents to kill the baby Oedipus. The Ancient Greeks recognised that parents are capable of murdering their offspring. The fear of infanticide held by children has its roots in reality. That fear will be all the more intense if the child has been abused, attacked and threatened. The child's hope of survival lies in parental love overcoming parental aggression, so the child has to make him or herself lovable and valuable to the parent. This may be achieved by accepting abuse without resistance and without causing problems:

> In most instances the patient convinced himself that his parents wanted to and were capable of loving him but that it was his worthlessness that made them hate him and even want to destroy him. The investment in this distortion seemed universal and reflected in the range of its expression the degree of terror experienced by the child and of the hope that as soon as he became worthy he would be loved. (Bloch, 1979, p. 11)

Abused children believe that they will survive if they can make themselves of value to their parents and can find a role for themselves in the family system. This may explain why some children accept being made the scapegoat or take over the parental role.

The sibling of an abused child or a child abused by siblings may well harbour the same fear of being killed and thus develop the same mistrust, sense of unworthiness and need to win parental love whatever the cost. Dorothy Bloch noted that it:

> did not need to be necessary for the child himself to be the target . . . violent and habitually attacking older siblings were experienced as agents of the

parents; where the parents didn't intervene effectively to protect the child, he assumed they wanted him killed. (Bloch, 1979, pp. 6–7)

Neglected children also have a realistic fear of death. Small children can die from starvation and from diseases associated with insanitary conditions and malnutrition. Children who are ignored are in danger, therefore youngsters may behave badly in order to attract attention. If they can feel a beating or hear a berating they know that they are alive and that someone is taking notice of them.

Finally, as the previous section on hostages indicated, victims can become paralysed by fear. A baby's 'frozen watchfulness' is one example. Erin Pizzey cites another:

> Ever since he was tiny, James has watched his mother suffer burning with a red hot poker, cigarettes stubbed out on her face, her legs slashed with knives, and his sister beaten before it was his turn. James is 9, and has been attending hospital for three years for depression. James is not a stupid child, he is just paralysed with fear, so he can barely read or write. (Pizzey, 1974)

This paralysis will result in the child's being unable to resist the abuser or exert any effort to seek assistance. Some will grow so quiet, almost mute, that they are literally unable to cry for help.

Doubt, shame and guilt

Abused children, riddled with fears, are mistrustful not only of other people but also of their own capabilities. They are trying to win the love of their parents but as long as the abuse continues they seem to be failing. They are full of doubts about themselves, and the safety of their environment. They therefore also doubt the ability of other people to rescue them, the ability of substitute parents to love them and the ability of the rest of the family to survive without them.

Shame is another enduring feeling of abused children. Firstly, there is the shame associated with being bad and in need of punishment. Beating, scolding and sending to bed without supper are all common ways of punishing misbehaviour. According to the straightforward logic of children, if they are severely beaten, berated or locked in a room without food it must be because they are very wicked. Bad behaviour and punishment is a source of shame and therefore a sense of shame pervades many abused youngsters.

Children who are intimidated or distressed can find it difficult to control their bowels and bladder and, once old enough to be toilet-trained, will be very ashamed of wetting or soiling themselves. To compound matters they are often told they are lazy, dirty and disgusting for doing so.

Other abusive practices can induce a sense of shame. Children at quite an early age learn that being naked and playing with private parts is seen as rude. A child who is smacked on the bare bottom may therefore be very embarrassed and humiliated, while a child persuaded or forced into sexual activities is also likely to feel ashamed.

Sexually abused children invariably feel that they are to blame for the abuse. Sometimes they enjoy the sexual activities or willingly accept the advances of the perpetrator because perhaps they are lonely. Sometimes they succumb to bribes. They may be made to feel to blame by the perpetrator accusing them of tempting and seducing him or her. The rest of the family, wishing to preserve the integrity of the perpetrator, may also blame the victim. Certain material designed to prevent sexual abuse may have the effect of compounding the guilt. Children are told to say 'no' to a sexual advance and tell someone. If they fail to do so they may feel they have disobeyed instructions. Adults tend to underestimate the courage needed to resist a powerful figure and to disclose distressing, embarrassing incidents.

Infants cry and, unless grossly neglected, are fed and tended to, they seem to have magical powers to control their environment. Consequently small children begin to feel responsible for whatever happens. 'With his concept of the magical nature of his thoughts, wishes and feelings, he may also assume responsibility for an extraordinary range of unhappy events' (Bloch, 1979, p. 5). Older children may have to contend with the feeling that they were old enough to have done something about events. All this adds to an abused child's feelings of guilt.

Children can also feel responsible for others. If they tell someone about the abuse their parents may be prosecuted or the family split up. The reason for so many retractions lies in the guilty feelings weighing on a child whose disclosure has led to such events. Youngsters who are removed into care may be unable to enjoy their new-found freedom from abuse because they believe that it was achieved at the expense of other family members.

Guilt may be induced in the child if the parents are abusive one moment and caring the next:

> When the parent is good the child feels guilty for the hatred it feels during the periods when the parent is bad. This is further complicated by strong feelings of compassion and pity because the parents look helpless and in need of the child's love and affection. When the parent is bad the child becomes full of hatred and contempt for the parent and for himself for being fooled yet again by compassion. (Pizzey, 1974)

Finally, children may be blamed for having provoked the abuser. There is still a strongly held belief in 'Lolitas', i.e. in teenage girls seducing 'innocent', unsuspecting males. In relation to physical abuse there is the concept of over-chastisement; the child has deserved punishment and provoked the parents so much that they have lost control. A constantly crying baby is regarded as provocative. In all these cases the child is seen as the agent of abuse, sympathy is reserved for the adult who claims to have been pushed beyond the limits of endurance.

Towards despair

The abused child develops a sense of unworthiness because of the feelings of shame and guilt evoked by mistreatment. This results in a sense of inferiority which is reinforced by the child's seeming inability to win parental approval and love. It follows that abused children may be reticent about seeking or accepting help; they conclude that if their parents do not think that they are worth protecting and loving there is no reason why any other adult would do so.

The fifth of Erikson's stages is identity versus role confusion. Inappropriate role adoption is a recognised aspect of child abuse. Children may accept the role of family scapegoat or victim in order to be of some value to the parents. They may moreover cling tenaciously to their role, fearing rejection, even annihilation if they lose it. This explains why abused children sometimes resist change and rescue. They know no other role and if removed from the family attempt to establish themselves as scapegoat and victim in their substitute families.

Role confusion also occurs when the child becomes responsible for family members and takes on a parental function. Ronald Summit discussing the way that children adapt to sexual abuse writes, 'the child, not the parent must mobilise the altruism and self-control to ensure the survival of the others' (Summit, 1983). This means that the child may feel bound to keep the family's secret whatever the cost in order to ensure the family is not split up. He or she may then be unsettled in care, worrying about what is happening to absent parents and siblings.

A sense of isolation, the sixth of Erikson's stages, is apparent in the accounts given by many abused children. They often feel different from their school fellows. They may be ashamed of their families or their condition. Furthermore abusive parents tend to discourage friendships. Abused children cannot be intimate with anyone outside the family owing to their feelings of guilt and shame. They will suspect genuine kindness because of their inability to trust and their sense of their own unworthiness and so they keep people at arm's length, carrying the burden of their secret alone.

Children who feel mistrustful and isolated will be heading towards stagnation and despair rather than being full of ideas for change and hope for the future. They will resist disclosure and removal from home because they may, in their despair, doubt that the situation will ever improve for them. Even when settled in a loving foster home they may expect things to deteriorate and will try to provoke the foster parents into abusing and rejecting them rather than wait for the inevitable (they believe) abuse and rejection to occur.

Abnormal learning

'Learned helplessness' is associated with despair. It is a term coined by psychologist, Martin Seligman. He demonstrated by laboratory experiments on rats and dogs that if animals are prevented from escaping they will eventually remain immobile even when given a real opportunity to escape. In further tests with human beings Seligman showed that when people believe that they have no control over the outcome of a response they will behave helplessly even when they do in fact have control (Seligman, 1975).

These experiments throw light on the behaviour of some abused children. Often abuse starts at an early age when youngsters cannot run away, speak up for themselves or draw attention to their plight in an effective manner. By the time they are old enough to do so they will have been subjected to the process of learned helplessness and will not seek help or use any opportunities for escape that present themselves.

Some victims of abuse do seek help but often in an indirect way. If time and again adults fail to understand the children's messages, they will give up hope of any help being forthcoming. Some children are able to ask for assistance directly but often they are not believed or nothing happens because the parents are unable to change and the legal grounds to force a change are absent. Children are then in a worse situation. Like Seligman's dogs, who were given shocks every time they attempted to escape, the youngsters will despair of receiving help. Consequently they may resist offers of help even when, eventually, someone with the power to intervene tries to do so.

Associated with learned helplessness and the process of learning is the concept of conditioning. American scientist, E. L. Thorndike (1913) found that cats can learn to pull a wire in order to reach food, this response was called 'operant conditioning'. In addition Thorndike developed the 'Law of Effect' in which he stated that when a response produces a reward or a feeling of satisfaction it will, in similar circumstances, be repeated. American psychologist, B. F.

Skinner (1953) demonstrated that if behaviour is rewarded or a threat removed the behaviour will be reinforced. He applied this to human beings. Skinner also noted that punishment weakens responses to stimuli.

Many adults use this theory, even if they have never heard of 'Stimulus Response Reinforcement', in the teaching of children. They naturally praise or reward desirable behaviour and punish undesirable behaviour. At a simple level this works; a toddler will not touch a hot kettle if he has been made uncomfortable either by being burnt or by being told sharply not to touch; he will say 'please' once he realises this results in his being given something that he wants.

However, people are more complicated than animals and learning in human beings is not such a simple process. We do not just avoid unpleasant stimuli and seek pleasant ones. We have consciences, imagination and principles which may over-ride simple conditioning; martyrs, for example, accept torture and death rather than renounce their beliefs. Similarly, abused children may accept pain and suffering rather than lose something less tangible. One abused child, Helen, accepted the pain of attempted intercourse rather than lose the attention of her brother; she went hungry and uncomfortable in an attempt to win her mother's love. Those outside the family may not understand why youngsters choose to remain at home even though they are likely to be beaten, molested or go hungry but it is because, to a child, some things such as security in what is familiar or the chance to win parental love are more important than mere avoidance of pain and discomfort.

Some neglected children fail to develop because their environment lacks stimulation, they are therefore unable to seek a change in their circumstances. Some emotionally and physically abused children are prevented from exploring their world and satisfying their curiosity because if they go beyond very tight limits or cause any disruption they will be punished. Eventually it becomes more expedient not to reach out, not to try anything different. They are therefore unwilling to seek a change in their circumstances.

Finally the youngsters may not seek help or removal from home because despite advancing in years the abuse results in their remaining emotionally like dependent infants. In some cases, especially those of neglect and physical abuse, this may be due to brain damage. But more often the retardation is of a less tangible nature. It will be recalled that hostage and concentration camp imprisonment result in regression in adults. A similar situation such as the abusive home is likely to produce regression or, if the youngster is too young to regress, failure to develop. Abused people sometimes remain emotionally dependent, clinging to their parents. If they do manage to leave home they become dependent on a partner who like their parents alternately cares for and abuses them. They also depend on their own children to meet their emotional needs and become frustrated when their offspring fail to do so. They thus become the next generation of abusive parents.

2

Voices of the Children

A number of abused children can ask for help in a firm direct manner and are able to describe their experiences clearly and coherently. But such youngsters are probably in the minority. Most are inhibited by the pressures described in the previous chapter. Moreover younger children do not have the command of language needed to communicate their distress in a straightforward manner. For these reasons the perspectives of the children are all too often ignored or misunderstood. Yet social workers and other professionals will fail to give effective help to children unless they can appreciate what the experience of abuse means for the victim. They also need to recognise how he or she may attempt to communicate that experience.

Insight into the world of the abused child is provided by adults who have suffered childhood mistreatment and are willing to describe their experiences. This chapter contains three such accounts. These illustrate some of the points raised in the previous chapter and serve as case examples to increase understanding of an abused child's predicament.

Marie's account

I lived with my mother, father, brother and sisters. Pauline was the eldest. Barry, my brother was two years younger than me and Linda was the youngest. My father was violent to my mother and all of his children.

Until I was eight years old our family seemed fairly 'normal'. There were rows but I was not aware of any extreme violence. My father was in the navy and away from home for quite long periods until I was aged about five. Despite the apparent normality of the situation there was already an atmosphere of fear in the house because my father was very strict. At bedtime he would look at the clock and whoever's turn it was to go to bed would scurry away.

After my eighth birthday came a dramatic change. My father had played with us giving us 'twizzles', swinging us around. My eldest sister then went to live with grandma. Us other children were asked a lot of questions by our mother. Father was also away at this time. When he came back there were lots of rows and we were not allowed to play the games with him any longer. One thing that puzzled me was that my mother gave us a strip wash in front of my father. I didn't know why but I found it very embarrassing; we had been taught to keep covered up in front of my father.

The situation went from bad to worse. I had the impression that something bad had happened. I heard sexual words like 'climax' for the first time but I didn't really understand what they meant. I remember Pauline being withdrawn and unhappy. A big black cloud descended over our house. We were not encouraged to have any friends. My father always found something wrong with them. Everything became very secretive. When my father went away to sea we became happy as a big weight was lifted but we all knew he would be coming back and the black void would return.

Our mother used to work hard. She would often cry. At nights I would go to bed then get up later, creep down, make mother a cup of tea and stay up with her until three or four in the morning when my father was away. I was very close to her and I knew this was a comfort to her. I was an eight-year-old comforting my mother.

This pattern continued until I was about eleven. Then we moved house. We hoped this would be a new beginning; things were going to be different and get better. But they weren't and from then on the situation was horrific. At around this time Pauline told me that our father had sexually abused her. He had done nearly everything except penetrate her. She wanted it to stop. He kept saying 'Have you come yet?' to her but she didn't know what he meant. Not long after this conversation Pauline ate a hundred aspirins in front of me. I didn't realise what was happing, I thought she was eating crumbly white cheese. She tried to commit suicide six times after this. I just didn't understand what she was going through. I was totally confused and afraid. When I did realise I felt it was my fault; I should have stopped her. My mother accompanied Pauline in the ambulance and she kept saying, 'Don't tell anyone why you did it. They will ask you but don't tell them'. These incidents seemed to have no effect on my father, he denied abusing Pauline, apart from the one earlier incident when I was eight.

Our father was often very violent. Frequently he had been drinking. On one occasion when I was outside the house and everyone else was inside, my father was on the rampage and had his hands round my mother's throat. A next-door neighbour called me over to her house and told me to listen. Through the walls I could hear someone shouting to get the police. The neighbour gave me a lift to the police station. I felt this was all I could do but I knew how violent my father could be. When the police arrived he tried to pretend it was just a domestic dispute. Us children ran out of the house and hid. The younger two kept singing 'They've come to take him away ha ha, he he'. Although the police arrested him he did not stay away for long.

On another occasion my father wanted money. He started throwing my mother's perfume and all her possessions about the house in a temper because she would not give him any. At the time I had a paper round; my mother told me to hide my money. My father asked me where it was. When I said that I had lost it he started hitting me. He also hit my mother and wrecked her bedroom, breaking up everything as he looked for money.

One Christmas a row started over something trivial. My father smashed a plant, a present for my mother, on to the kitchen floor. It made a mess with the soil and broken pot. He threw a large box of chocolates on top. He then made the younger children take the baubles off the tree and threw them into the kitchen too. My mother aimed an ash tray at my father. It missed but caused a hole in the wall. He, in retaliation, cut her leg with a broken dinner plate. The other children were crying and he slammed out. I was left picking up the pieces and I helped to bathe my mother's leg.

I always used to calm the others and tried to look after them. Pauline would go to her room and she became increasingly withdrawn. Linda would switch off and block out what was happening. Barry never seemed to be around, he managed to 'duck out'. I sometimes used to hide with him in the cellar. It was however usually my mother, brother and myself who had the good hidings. Our father used to hit us with anything – his belt, his fist or kick us with his boots. Once I was so black and blue that mum was going to send me to my grandparents. When I was bruised I was kept off school until the bruises faded.

The night times were bad. Us girls shared a room. I used to be awake a lot particularly because I would try to comfort my mother by going to her to hold her hand. We would hear my father's key then I would quickly clamber back to bed and pretend I was asleep. My father would creep into our room, ostensibly to tuck us in but he seemed to be trying to see who was in the deepest sleep. Sometimes he would stay by our bedside for two minutes, sometimes for fifteen. At that stage he didn't touch me but there was always the fear, the dread, wondering if it was going to be my turn. If one of the other two woke he would say, 'Shh, you're only dreaming go back to sleep'. Living in fear was the worst thing. One night he dragged me out of bed at one o'clock because I hadn't cleaned his shoes. He started hitting me and made me clean them in the middle of the night. My mother tried to defend me saying, 'I'll do it, she's got to go to school tomorrow'.

I couldn't mix in school; I used to sit alone. From thirteen years onwards I played truant continually. We were cut off from the other children for fear of letting anything slip. I was dying to tell someone who would take me away. Someone kind who would understand, but then I used to think, 'How would my mother and the others cope without me?' I felt it was me who held them together. We always appeared clean and tidy. We were not allowed to wear make-up or be fashionable and we felt different from everyone else. We knew too much. I felt so very alone, totally alone.

You can't concentrate at school while wondering what will happen when you get home. I was very wary of all the male teachers. I couldn't learn from them because of the need to put up all the defences. I assumed that underneath they were all like my father and I was hostile to them. I tried to be helpful to the women teachers. I used to sit wondering if they were battered at home too. I also wondered what other children's lives were like at home. I once went to another girl's house and I couldn't believe how nice her mum and dad were and thought why aren't mine like that?

We would swing from a semi-normal life when my father was away and we could have friends including boyfriends, to a state of fear when he came back. It was difficult to have friends because they couldn't understand why I was friendly one moment and suddenly distant the next. It was easier not to have friends, so I became isolated. I couldn't tell people what was happening at home, they wouldn't believe me or they would misunderstand what I was saying. I began to try to predict what my father would do, try to get to know the enemy and stay one jump ahead of him.

As we grew older we used to devise signals. For example if our father was out we would leave the outside light on for our boyfriends. If the light was off then they must come nowhere near the house. We explained to the boys that we just had a rather over-protective father. Our mother knew everything. I could tell her anything. She would be frightened for us. She had a terrible time, stuck in the middle. Mother stayed with our father because she loved him. She did leave him once but not for long. I feel there is nothing lovable about him. In some ways I'm angry with my mother for staying while knowing what he did to us.

Pauline and I often wondered how we did not end up in an asylum, having to live with all that fear and violence and the constant threat of sexual abuse. My main feeling was to try to make it easier for everyone else. I used to clean the house from top to bottom, do all the ironing and get the youngsters out of the house as much as possible to be away from my father. He was really hard on Barry who could not stand up to him. He kept starting fires and stealing. Father used to just give him a good hiding.

I was sexually abused by my father when I was 21 years old. I had married but my husband was violent and sexually abusive so I went back to live with my parents. It was then that my father attempted to have sex with me although he did not manage to penetrate. I could hardly believe what was happening. I had escaped during childhood then all of a sudden my nightmare came true.

Helen's account

I should perhaps have been a happy child, after all I lived in a big house with plenty of food, toys and pretty clothes. I had a father who enjoyed being with me, a mother whom I loved and a brother whom I thought wonderful.

Frank, my brother, was five years older than me and was a quiet, studious boy. My father was warm-hearted and jovial but he was not at home very much because he would commute daily to London spending long hours at his office or would be abroad on business trips. My mother did not go out to a paid job but she was always very busy. She spent much of her time supporting children's charities.

My mother seemed to be devoted to children. She expended so much energy on fund-raising for deprived and cruelly treated children. But I knew that she didn't love me. That must have been, I concluded, because I was such a horrible, unlovable child. It never occurred to me that perhaps the problem lay with my mother who was attracted to the sentimental image of children but could not abide the real thing. It was only gradually that I realised that she did not like Frank very much either.

I used to try so hard to be good so that she would love me. She used to tell me how lucky I was to have a nice house and pretty clothes. I longed to be poor, I thought I might be more lovable if I was destitute. I used to wear only my oldest clothes. My mother had a struggle to make me wear any of my newer, more attractive dresses. I used to deny myself sweets and would not spend my pocket money on myself. I used to pretend whenever possible that I was poor. I would hide from school friends that fact that we had a car, holidays abroad and other trappings of affluence. I was ashamed of our big house and would not invite friends home in case they saw that I was not poor.

Wearing shabby clothes in fact irritated my mother because she was a smart woman obsessed with neatness, order and cleanliness. I could not really play freely in the house or garden because everything had to remain tidy and spotless. Even my dolls had to be arranged in serried ranks. If my mother found a toy out of place she would confiscate it. The only doll she never bothered with was Penny, my scruffy rag doll with only one arm and a bald head. I loved Penny dearly because she was really mine. All the others I regarded as my mother's to take and give back as she chose.

If, when I was young, I was so ill that I had to stay off school my mother was very angry with me. It meant that she either had to cancel a meeting to stay with me or pay for a baby-sitter. I tried very hard not to have days off school so that when I had flu I would sit sweating and nearly fainting in the classroom and shivering uncontrollably in the playground at break-time. When I did have to have days away from school I had to stay in bed and sleep or read all day. When the baby-sitter was used I would hear my mother come back home after a meeting. I would cry out to her. I just wanted to see her yet she would not come upstairs. I eventually stopped calling for her and just sobbed quietly. My brother would often bring me my tea. Eventually, sometime during the evening, my mother would come in and ask me angrily what I had been making a fuss about.

At night I had to go to bed, switch off the light and go straight to sleep. Often I could not go to sleep immediately but I would not dare to get out of bed and switch the light on. I would lie there terrified because I could hear the floorboards creak outside my door and I was sure that a man with a gun was coming in to shoot me. I sat staring at the door for ages waiting in fear for the man to come.

My fears were relieved a little when I was about six because Frank started to come to my room in the evening to cuddle me. We did not switch on my light but could see dimly by the glow of a lamp shining through my window. I loved Frank's reassuring embraces and felt so grateful to him. I thought that the man with the gun would not come in with Frank there. I looked forward to his visits. I knew that I was being naughty because I should have been asleep. I also sensed that Frank thought he was doing something wrong because when he heard our parents come upstairs he would dash out. The toilet was next to my bedroom so that if they saw him coming from the direction of my room they would assume he had been to the toilet. Often he would have time to flush it.

As time passed the cuddles became closer. Frank would take off my nightie and come in wearing just his dressing-gown which he would also take off. He would rub me between the legs. I liked this and he made me feel special. Then he started to practise different ways of kissing me which I didn't like so much. He also simulated intercourse rubbing his penis between my legs. He told me it was allright because it was what 'Mummies and daddies do to get babies'. I still didn't like it. I felt the weight of his body squashing mine and I could smell his excited sweat as I struggled to find a breathing space in the gap under his armpit between his arm and his chest.

One problem that emerged at this time was that Frank seemed to get excited and wet my bed a little. I used to cover the patch with a towel so that I did not have to go to sleep lying in the damp part but I was always apprehensive in case in the mornings my mother or father pulled back the sheets too far and saw the towel or the patch. I realised that the sheets were messy so I began to volunteer to help make the beds including my own and would change my own sheets at the weekends.

As we grew older Frank's demands increased. He started to attempt full intercourse. It hurt me so much but I could not scream out loud in case my parents heard. I just had to scream inside my head. I had a re-occurring nightmare of screaming and screaming but knowing no one could hear me or help me. Frank also wanted to experiment in other ways, anally and orally. I hated this but he threatened to spank me if I refused. I didn't realise that this would probably not have been possible in the circumstances, all I knew from the occasional spankings my father had given me that they were noisy, painful, humiliating affairs that I wanted to avoid at all costs. I also wanted Frank to love me which could be best achieved by pleasing him.

I began to realise that what we were doing might result in pregnancy. Frank explained that that would not happen until I started having monthly periods. These started when I was thirteen. Frank then stopped coming to my room partly because it coincided with his leaving home to start at college and partly because he now had a girlfriend, something he had not had in his earlier teens because he had been so painfully shy, uncertain of himself and isolated. He had been unloved by our mother and put under pressure by our father who had high hopes for his only son. In some ways I felt sad and rejected when Frank stopped coming to my room. I had wanted some of the sexual activities to stop but he had made me feel special and important to him, now he took little notice of me.

I was terrified for both myself and for Frank in case our secret was discovered. I would not let anyone get close to me in case they 'saw through me' and found out what I was really like – a dirty, rude, little girl. My father still wanted to cuddle me when he was at home but I held him at arm's length, in case he came so close that he saw how dirty I was. Once, as I backed off from him, I caught the hurt look in his eyes. I felt unworthy of his affection.

At school I appeared to be reasonably popular. I was naturally very good at most sports therefore my class mates always wanted me in their team. I learnt to strum a guitar which also helped in my teens. But inside I felt so isolated, I was different from the others. I had done something so wicked that I deserved a dreadful punishment. I tried to be good and work hard in order to avoid any punishment. I could not bear being given a bad conduct mark at school as it only served to confirm how dreadful I was.

I also tried to work hard because I thought that by getting high marks my mother would love me because she was always delighted when Frank did well academically. As a teenager my isolation increased. My fellow pupils used to jeer at me because I was regarded as so naive about sexual matters. The others would gather in little groups to read the 'juicy bits' of various salacious novels, I did not join in because I was frightened that I might 'let something slip' and show that I knew too much. I also didn't have boyfriends because I could not abide the feeling of being experimented upon by an inexperienced youth.

Even after the sexual abuse stopped I still carried a weighty secret and felt unclean and guilty. I wore clean clothes every day. I tried to eat very little. The reasons for this were various. I needed to be in control of my own body, while forbidding myself food was a form of punishment. Moreover I feared being sexually attractive and being molested again. Finally, I suppose I was still trying to make myself into one of those emaciated children for whom my mother seemed to feel such affection.

Sarah's account

I actually decided fairly early on that I didn't like my father which is a big decision for a child. It was because I was frightened of his strict discipline and use of corporal punishment but I also hated the way he treated my mother. My younger sister, Barbara and I used to compete not to sit behind him in the car because we could not bear to be that close to him.

I used to get spanked a lot. He was a headmaster and I went to his school. The role of father and headmaster became muddled but I didn't realise anything was wrong I just thought that what he did was what all teachers did. I was isolated and had no comparison of my family life with any other.

My father used to tell me not to put my hands in my pockets because it was, in his opinion, slovenly. Once I was at my grandparent's when my father arrived. He caught me with my hands in my pockets. He saw this as an act of defiance although in fact I had been playing happily and hadn't realised what I was doing. He grabbed me, bundled me into the car, took me home and beat me. My grandmother had cried and pleaded with him not to hurt me but he brushed her out of the way. After he had beaten me I was heart-warmed to find my other grandmother sitting on the stairs weeping because of the way I had been treated.

He bullied everyone either in a straightforward way or by using a judicious combination of good-looks, charm and manipulation. He was used to having his own way. I accepted the fact he had a right to hit me. The beatings hurt and I wanted them to stop. The pain didn't leave a lot of space in my mind for any other thoughts. I was very miserable afterwards feeling rejected, cast out, punished, not worthy. The effect of this situation was to make life such that, because punishment might happen at any time, no day was a safe day, a good day, until it was over. I resented not owning my life.

Besides the beatings my father used other strange ways of punishing us, for example he would put us in the car then drive very fast to teach us a lesson. I can remember the liberation that came when I was eighteen and was so unhappy that I didn't care whether I lived or died. This meant that when he drove fast he could no longer frighten me. I found that experience almost exhilarating.

One New Year there was a party next door. Both my parents drank heavily. I came back with my father and sister but the following morning my mother still hadn't returned. There was thick snow on the ground. My father told me that my mother was probably dead and sent me out to look everywhere, under all the hedges, for her body. I still carry the horror of that episode. She had in fact stayed overnight with the people next door but I didn't realise that and believed my father.

I always felt that if anything happened to my mother I wouldn't know what to do. Whatever kindness came from our home was from her. I always thought of her as my father's first victim and myself as second. I was distressed by the way I had to witness his treatment of my mother. He would constantly undermine her – for example, she was once enjoying music on the car radio when my father decided to stop the car and get out. He switched off the radio saying that he had to save the batteries. Even as a young child I realised it had nothing to do with batteries. Another time, on holiday, my mother sat on a wall and standing up had some tar on her skirt. My father shouted 'God, woman, you've sh. . . .d yourself as usual'. Yet he constantly told us how beautiful she was and how lucky we were to have her as a mother. This, however, struck me as false.

I felt protective towards my mother. She was fascinated by my father and even when they finally separated she never became a whole person' again. She needed to be fighting disasters and crises. She couldn't accept herself and turned more and more to drink. She was so unhappy that a lot of me parented her, I tried to cheer her up. It was only as a parent myself that I became angry that she never protected us. I have never told her how angry I felt.

I remember truly hating my sister. My father used to say to me 'Why can't you be like your sister, she's gregarious, has lots of friends and is cheerful? You are just a sour puss.' I was jealous of her. I did not realise he said the same to her about me, making her jealous as well. I could not afford to protect her. When I eventually decided to leave home, my father threatened me with the fact that Barbara would be made to suffer because I was not there. But I had to close my mind to that. I used however to draw his fire because, when I dared, I stood up to him. I now only have a superficial relationship with my sister.

He made me have my hair cut very short like a boy so I wore headscarves. He said by doing this I was trying to look like 'a duchess', trying to show that I was better than the rest of the family. Once, when we were having a picnic, he made me sit some distance from the family in a field by myself to eat. I cringed up inside. He always made us feel he was in the right. In order to escape I used to day-dream. One place that could be mine was inside my head, but he even resented this. We were in the car when I was imagining the dog I would give my grandmother for a present. I was hauled out of my reverie by father shouting, 'Look at that bloody, snotty cow in the back, too hoity-toity to talk to the rest of us'. His verbal attack was vitriolic. Another time when I wore a new bathing costume and felt quite proud of it he shouted across a quiet beach, 'Hold your belly in woman, you look like a pregnant cow'.

I was eleven years old and the only girl in my father's school. As the headmaster's daughter I was not popular. I felt very isolated but in a desperate attempt to gain popularity I became involved in some sex play with the boys. When I heard that my father had found out I fainted with fear. I was also frightened of one of the boys and so I withheld his name from my father who, when he discovered this, made me change into some of his thin rugby shorts. Then he caned me really hard. Half way through he showed my mother my bottom and she was sick then he carried on caning me. A fortnight later when my mother jokingly patted my bottom I cried out because the pain was still so intense.

I asked my mother if I would have to go away after this incident. She said 'Yes, perhaps'. I thought I would just be thrown out of the house into the proverbial darkness. I wondered if I could live in a cave that I knew about in the mountain and hoped someone would put out food for me. In fact I was sent to boarding school although it was the summer term. I was very unhappy. I cried so much at bed-time that the staff had to intervene. They thought I was homesick, missing a loving family but I was crying because I felt rejected and did not seem to belong to anyone. Because I started in the summer term friendships were already made in that year and yet by the next term I did not belong in the new intake. I made no real friends.

My father kept telling me that if I didn't achieve high academic results I would be sent to a state school implying that I would be virtually 'chucked in the bin'. I spent my time on the fringes wishing I had the confidence and the time to socialise. My father kept me short of money so I could not join in any school activities that cost money. I tried to tell some of my school-mates about my home life but generally they did not believe me. My father was handsome and charming and when he came to school the pupils would all try to catch a glimpse of him and say how lucky I was. I was so grateful to one friend who stayed with us for a while and, realising what I had been saying was true, told me she believed me. I used to look forward to going home for the holidays because I always hoped that this time the nightmare would end and we would be an ordinary family.

As a teenager I was subjected to sexual bullying. He used to take me out making comments such as, 'People will think you are my girl friend'. He would have a lot to drink. On the way back he would stop the car and fondle me. I could smell the drink on his breath. I did not believe I could say 'no' to him so I just used to freeze. When I tried to refuse to masturbate him he said that I shouldn't get married because I was frigid and any man who took me on would be getting a poor deal. I wished he wouldn't do it and I felt guilty because I thought that I was letting my mother down and committing an infidelity. He would describe to me the merits of various women with whom he had affairs.

When I was seventeen I met a man many years older than myself and fell deeply in love with him. Perhaps in an attempt to escape from home I became engaged to him. He was a man very like my father. He found another girl friend, the engagement was broken. I was devastated. But other people didn't let me down. Aged eighteen I decided to leave home for good. My father threatened me in order to keep me from leaving. My mother rang my uncle and aunt. I took a bus to their home and my uncle met me at the bus stop. They took me into their home and made me feel valued and cared for. When I was ready to move on they let me go.

Cries for help

The three accounts in this chapter were all given by adults. It is generally harder for children to talk so directly and clearly about their experiences. The reasons why that should be so were examined in the previous chapter. However, children indicate their distress in a variety of ways and many of these are outlined below.

Verbal communication

Small children who have learned to talk but who cannot fully appreciate the consequences of what they say may describe their abuse spontaneously. This can, however, go unrecognised. 'Daddy tickles me with his hammer' may be dismissed as childish nonsense. Sometimes children do not have the words to describe their experiences so they make words up. One little boy kept saying that 'Uncle Harry gooed on me'. It was only with careful questioning that he was able to indicate that he had been sexually abused and had been trying to describe the way the perpetrator ejaculated on him. A small child often has difficulty indicating the degree of the abuse so a child may say, 'Mummy smacked me and made me sad' which could equally mean that the mother administered a mild slap or that she lashed out harshly and recklessly for no good reason. Small children may also lack clarity in their enunciation leaving adults unsure whether the youngster is saying something like 'Daddy showed me his willie' or 'Danny showed me his wellie'.

Another problem encountered by practitioners trying to investigate allegations of abuse by very young children is that often they will tell one person then, having unburdened themselves, will not talk about the abuse again for quite a long time. Older children can often be encouraged to repeat what they have said to people who can help them; younger ones are not so open to such persuasion.

Older youngsters may be able to articulate what has happened to them but are more aware of possible consequences. They sometimes start to tell somebody in a manner that gives them a way out if they change their mind and also tests the reactions of the person in whom they confide. They may therefore start with a question such as, 'What is meant by intercourse' or by a statement such as, 'I don't really want to go home this afternoon'.

Children may find that they are not believed as happened in the case of Sarah who had such a superficially charming father. They rarely lie about abusive experiences within the family. Nevertheless they may make up stories about their home background as exemplified by Helen who pretended that she was poor. But if these stories are negative ones they may well be indicators of some form of abuse, albeit not the mistreatment described.

It is not unusual for children to retract their allegations. This does not usually mean that they were originally lying. The commonest reason is that they cannot cope with the consequences of disclosure, especially if the family is disrupted and its members reject the child. He or she may feel that a retraction will result in the family being reunited and everything 'being all right'.

Physical appearance

There are a number of physical indicators of abuse which can amount to a cry for help on the part of a youngster. Sometimes abused children will draw attention to a physical injury in a straightforward way. They may have had enough and want the abuse to stop whatever the consequences. Sometimes they may indicate an injury indirectly in the hope that someone will notice their discomfort, examples include wincing dramatically when they sit down or saying that they cannot do games because their leg hurts. More usually children will try to cover up injuries and if they are asked about them will give an explanation which is inconsistent with the injuries. A child with bruises on the inside and outside the thighs and on both sides of the face is unlikely to have sustained them all by falling off a bicycle. Patterns of absence from nursery or school should be noted if there is any suspicion of abuse because, as happened in the case of Marie, children may be kept at home until injuries heal.

Physically and sometimes emotionally neglected children will show physical signs. A poorly clad, dirty, emaciated youngster will be readily spotted. A baby putting on very little weight and a child who is obviously stunted in growth will also merit examination. However, clothing can often mask an underweight child. One little girl always wore long, loose dresses and thick cardigans. It was only when the teacher picked the girl up to sit her on her knee that she felt how very much lighter she was than all the other pupils. Babies often have naturally chubby faces which belie an emaciated body.

The child's facial expression and body movements can be indicators of abuse. Distressed babies will usually cry, however some infants who have been persistently attacked will show 'frozen watchfulness'. The baby will have a fixed smile and his eyes will follow adults around in a wary manner. He will not laugh, cry and gurgle in a spontaneous way. Older children may look apprehensive and again lack spontaneity in the presence of adults.

Behavioural signs

The reactions of children to abuse can vary to a considerable extent. It is therefore difficult to list the various behaviours which might be symptomatic of abuse. However there are some which are worth considering. A sudden change of behaviour can be significant; for example the normally outgoing child who becomes withdrawn or the quiet, well-behaved child who becomes noisy and demanding. Unfortunately such changes are often dismissed as a 'phase the child is going through'.

Extremes of good or bad behaviour may also be an indication of mistreatment at home. Helen was so concerned not to be thought of as bad that her behaviour in school was exemplary. Many abused children truant from school because they feel so different from other children. They are ashamed of what is happening and want to hide away from the world. Sometimes they are forced to stay away to look after younger siblings.

Small children who have been sexually abused may act out their experiences with other children or toys. Nursery staff often recognise that youngsters who pull other children's pants down, trying to mount them as if to have intercourse are going beyond the normal games of 'mummies and daddies'. Older children may become promiscuous or, as in Helen's case, show extreme naivety and lack of interest in sexual matters. Suicide attempts can be associated with sexually abused adolescents, as are eating disorders.

Children who are subjected to physical or verbal violence in the home are likely to show aggressive behaviour and bully other children. Alternatively they may be very passive and seem to invite the attentions of the school bully.

Finally children may show no extremes or oddities of behaviour because they compartmentalise their lives. They metaphorically put the abuse into a separate box and forget about it during the times when it is not occurring. Nevertheless, there will be faint clues as most abused children feel isolated, unworthy and afraid. Perhaps the youngster will day-dream a lot, be forgetful – the memory works overtime to blank out bad experiences – or be rather tired as night-time abuse and nightmares take their toll.

3

Individual Work with Children

To 'rescue' abused children by removing them from the source of abuse is not enough. To 'reform' the parents, working with them to alter their abusive behaviour is also not enough. If abused children are to be helped they must be released from the misconceptions, false learning and negative emotions described in the previous chapters. These imprison them in a world of fear, mistrust, self-denigration and isolation long after the abuse itself has stopped.

Some children will present themselves as severely disturbed. These youngsters will require skilled psychotherapy. It is not the purpose of this book to teach social workers about psychotherapy. It requires specialist training which the majority of social workers do not have. Children needing this form of treatment should be referred to an agency which provides a skilled service. However the majority of abused children and their siblings can be helped through various forms of therapy which are within the capabilities of many social workers.

The word 'therapist' is used to indicate the person who is offering structured, direct help to enable the child to come to terms with what has happened. This help can embrace a variety of methods based on a wide range of theoretical perspectives. The term should not be confused with the word 'psychotherapist', which usually indicates a purely psychoanalytic approach.

The focus of this chapter is not so much on the investigative process it is more concerned with the therapeutic needs of youngsters once an investigation has clarified the situation. However investigative and therapeutic work are closely allied, so much so that a well-conducted investigation should start to help to release the child. It should be undertaken with great sensitivity to the feelings of the victim, account being taken of processes such as the 'Stockholm syndrome' which may complicate matters. Conversely therapeutic interviews can become the start of an investigation if during therapy a child discloses that the severity of the abuse was greater than first thought or that other adults and children were involved in the abusive activities. Many of the suggestions therefore will apply as much to investigative work as to therapy.

Requirements of the therapist

This chapter is addressed to social workers, especially those who have limited resources in terms of time, training, space and equipment. However it is acknowledged that there are other professionals who could undertake this work such as health visitors, nursery nurses and teachers. Moreover practitioners working with children who are not abused but who are nevertheless suffering distress may find some of the proposals in this chapter useful.

There are two opposing views of the type of people able to help abused children. At one extreme it is held that only 'experts' should be allowed to work with them, at the other extreme it is maintained that anyone can do so. Certainly some expertise is required but this can be acquired by workers with skills in other areas which are transferable to child abuse cases. But not everyone can undertake direct work with children and anybody who feels uncomfortable or distressed doing so should bow out gracefully. Children can readily sense an uneasy adult and will believe that they are the source of that unease; this will only serve to compound the youngster's feelings of guilt and unworthiness.

The most important requirement of any worker is that he or she should be comfortable with children and adolescents. Therapists should not object to sitting, kneeling, even lying on the floor. They should not mind biscuit crumbs and paint falling on their clothes. They should be tolerant of displays of violent behaviour and strings of swear words emanating from a child's mouth. Some male workers feel awkward with dolls and other toys traditionally associated with little girls and may need time playing with these before attempting any play therapy. A lively imagination, inventiveness and a willingness to learn from the child are additional requirements. Above all the worker must respect children and acknowledge that they should be given the same dignity, the same value and the same right to know what is happening to them as is given to adults.

An ability to communicate with children is obviously required. Simply talking may be adequate when counselling adults but is insufficient with children and with many adolescents. Youngsters communicate through play, spontaneous body language and actions.

On the other hand even young children appreciate the opportunity to talk, ask questions, and listen to explanations. One eight-year-old began a therapy session by asking if he could 'talk first and play later'.

A knowledge of normal child development will help in the choice of age-appropriate toys and activities. Abusive parents often expect too much of their offspring, therefore workers would only add to the youngster's self-doubt if they also demanded too much. A therapist who has a good knowledge of child development will also be able to assess how far a youngster's developmental progress has been impaired, which may indicate how much help is required.

Skills in helping bereaved people, especially children, through the process of grief and mourning can be transferred to work with abused children. Mistreated youngsters have suffered a whole host of losses: of self-esteem, of dignity, of security, of ability to trust, of un-conditional parental love, of sibling companionship and of part of their childhood. Loss reactions can be seen in abused children and their siblings. Denial, guilt, anger, sleep disorders, repression, isolation and helplessness are among the emotions and responses that the bereaved and the abused hold in common.

Working with abused children requires emotional resilience. Some adults may find the pain of the child unbearable. This can result in their avoiding discussion of the abusive activities and other distres-sing areas, always keeping the interview on a superficial level. Because of this the child may be left feeling that he or she has been involved in something so dreadful that it cannot be discussed. Children should be allowed to talk about the abuse and examine what it has meant for them. Moreover practitioners unable to bear the pain shown by a victim may blame him. This is because there is a process by which we find the suffering of others more bearable if we hold victims in some way responsible for their own fate. A number of adults may reject both the abuse and the abused child because the two are so inextricably bound together.

Difficulties may arise because some workers were themselves abused in childhood. Subconsciously the distress of the client becomes their own distress. But those who have been able to come to terms with their experiences may have valuable insights to offer. Workers who were not abused do not have this advantage and may have difficulty understanding the perspectives of their clients. Nevertheless, their relative objectivity can be of value, as long as they are able to use their imagination, powers of observation and natural sensitivity to respond appropriately.

Therapists who are themselves parents may find the mistreatment suffered by children similar to their own hard to cope with objectively. Alternatively they may over-identify with the abused child's parents particularly if they come from the same social group or the child behaves in a way that any adult would find difficult to tolerate. However practitioners who are parents may be more comfortable in the company of children and more readily recognise unreasonable parental behaviour.

The gender of the worker requires careful consideration. A child abused by a woman may be unable to tolerate a female worker, conversely a youngster who has only experienced female company may be uneasy with a male worker. In the initial stages the child's wishes and fears should be met by the choice of a worker of the appropriate gender. Later the child can be introduced to a worker of the opposite sex, thereby learning that not all people of the feared gender are abusive and uncaring.

Male workers sometimes voice concerns about working with very young children or teenage girls. However, many men are able to work effectively with both groups. Spending time helping in a day nursery or youth club and practising skills through role-play with colleagues may give him the confidence and competence that he needs.

One fear, particularly in relation to sexually abused children, is that they will falsely accuse a male worker of molesting them. This is unlikely to happen as very few youngsters tell lies about sexual abuse. Nevertheless children who have learnt that all relationships with men lead to sexual activities, may misinterpret actions by the therapist. Considerable sensitivity is needed to predict what actions may be unacceptable to a particular client. To overcome unwarranted accusations the sessions could be witnessed by a supervisor using a video monitor or a one-way screen. If such facilities are not available an ordinary audio recorder could be used to tape the sessions. A supervisor should then note the time the session started and finished and listen to the recording as soon as possible afterwards; although not a perfect solution, it provides some measure of protection for both therapist and child. Another option is for two adults to be in the room with the client. This has disadvantages because the outnumbering can prove daunting and inhibiting for some children.

Whether the therapists are male or female, young or old, married or single, new to the work or experienced they all require a competent, supportive supervisor. Occasionally workers, who have forgotten their own childhood mistreatment, will start to recall it because a client's distress can be a powerful reminder of their own. This can be very difficult for them to handle, so difficult that suicide is a very real risk. In these cases the supervisor should be prepared to listen and discuss with them the impact of their experiences but should not offer direct therapy. Instead he or she should help the workers find an acceptable counsellor. A supervisor trying to act as therapist will create considerable role confusion. Furthermore the needs of the client may be neglected in the face of the overwhelming emotional demands of the person being supervised.

Planning individual work

Much therapeutic effort, particularly in relation to physical abuse and neglect, has been directed towards the parents or the family as a whole. There is however a need for individual work with abused children and non-abused siblings. Such work may take place before, or in conjunction with other forms of therapy such as family or group work. One-to-one work is directed towards: (i) allowing expression of feelings in a safer context than in a family or group session, (ii) communicating positive messages to the child, (iii) enabling the child adopt new roles and (iv) teaching youngsters that they have a right not to be abused in future.

Individual work can vary in depth, content and setting. A severely neglected child may require many sessions simply learning to respond to stimuli and to play with toys and relate to one person before they can cope with any other help. Some older teenagers may welcome counselling and the opportunity to talk with no play element whereas others may welcome the opportunity to play freely and recapture some of their lost childhood. Individual therapy will therefore have to be tailored to the individual. The suggestions in the rest of this chapter should only be followed after the specific needs of each client have been considered. Before individual work can start there is the planning stage which includes such matters as duration, frequency, choice of personnel and location.

Duration and frequency

Duration applies both to the number of sessions and to their length. A single session only is worse than none. Children who share some aspects of themselves which they feel are shameful who are then not offered a follow-up session may conclude that they have shown themselves to be so awful that the worker does not want to see them again. Usually a minimum of four sessions is required but however many are planned there should be provision for an extra meeting in case the child reveals something unpleasant in the final planned session. The worker can use the additional meeting to show the youngster that he or she is still liked and accepted while the worker has not been put off or destroyed by the information revealed.

When the sessions have lasted beyond six months it is worth assessing whether or not they are meeting the child's needs or whether he or she would benefit from the deeper experience of pyschotherapy or the wider experience of a therapeutic group.

At least two hours will have to be allocated for each session. An initial period should be set aside for the therapist's mental and emotional preparation. Furthermore, even if he or she is fortunate enough to have access to a proper playroom, time will be needed in order to ensure that materials appropriate for the particular child are to hand. After the session it will take at least half an hour for the worker to assess, evaluate and record what has happened. He or she should also be allowed some time to relax and unwind before starting on the next task. This leaves approximately one hour for the session. It may be shorter especially in the early stages if the child is uneasy in the one-to-one situation. It may be longer when a youngster needs time to settle. There is however no point in prolonging sessions if a child is reluctant to respond, in the hope that eventually he or she will do so. It is better to stop the interview at the appointed time. The youngster may be more forthcoming during a later meeting when he or she may feel more comfortable.

Sessions will obviously be longer if the worker chooses an activity such as taking the child out for a meal. Such excursions can provide new stimuli for neglected children who have not had experience of them. However they can provide a relaxing environment for those youngsters for whom such activities are familiar.

Sessions are usually held once a week, preferably on the same day at the same time. Some youngsters benefit, particularly in the early stages, from having the frequency increased to two or three times a week. This is especially true of the young child for whom time passes slowly and who needs to build up a comfortable relationship with the helping adult as quickly as possible. Towards the end of therapy, sessions may gradually tail off by being held once a fortnight particularly if family or group work is planned to take the place of individual interviews.

Allocating tasks

If transport is needed to ferry the child to the session it is preferable that the therapist is not expected to drive. It can seem economical for one person to undertake both tasks but workers need all their energy for the therapeutic session. Some workers report that clients talk to them more readily in the car. This however usually indicates that there is something wrong with the interview. Perhaps the youngster does not like a lot of eye-contact when talking – in which case communication can be through a pretend telephone or sitting side by side. Perhaps the child feels more secure that conversations will not be overheard in the car – in which case the child can test the sound-proofing of the interview room or play background music to counter the fear of being overheard. Another reason why a worker should not double as a driver is that the session then lacks a proper start and finish. Beginnings and endings are important in all forms of therapy.

A careful decision has to be taken over whether or not the worker is also to be involved with other members of the family or with a group to which the children or their relatives belong. The worker may find that there are conflicts of loyalty if he or she helps other family members, on the other hand there may be conflicts with colleagues if he or she does not. There are forms of supervision and case management models of working which can help resolve these dilemmas; they will be discussed in the next chapter.

Location and environment

Sometimes there are good reasons for undertaking individual work in the child's own home. But often it is more appropriate to use an alternative location because in the family home children may feel the ties of loyalty binding them more tightly, preventing them from disclosing further abuse or from expressing anger against family members. In a foster home or residential setting the children may wish to distance themselves from their former unhappy experiences and will not want them introduced into their new environment. If work has to be undertaken in a residential or foster home, then unless the youngsters make a specific request to do so, their own bedroom should not be used. They should be allowed to preserve an area where they can relax without the intrusion of painful reminders.

The interview room should be comfortable, sound-proof and not a thoroughfare for other staff. If it is to be used with young children the floor should have a clean, soft covering. It must also be physically safe with, where necessary, protections such as a fireguard or electric socket covers. Easy chairs, a coffee table and cushions are all useful. If play work is to be undertaken then too few toys are better than too many. It is important that the child should not be overwhelmed and distracted by an abundance of play equipment. Spare toys should be kept out of sight in bags hanging from hooks high on a wall, in a locked cupboard or in plain cardboard boxes well out of reach. When there is a television present which the worker does not intend to use, experience has shown that removal of the aerial is a wise precaution.

If possible there should be easy access to a sink and toilet as well as to a room where a familiar adult accompanying the child can wait. It is also preferable that the same room looking more or less the same is used for each session.

Starting the session

When children first arrive they should be introduced to anyone they do not already know and then be given time to familiarise themselves with the geography of the building, unless of course sessions are held in their school or other places familiar to them. It is important to check that the children know the whereabouts of a hand-basin and toilet.

The next step is to ensure that the child does not feel isolated and trapped with the worker. This is particularly important in sexual abuse cases where the child might have been closeted in a room with an adult who is focusing on sexual matters. The similarities between the abusive and therapeutic scenarios might lead the child to feel that he or she may be abused again, this time by the worker. The child may be reassured by people monitoring the situation through a video or screen but more effective is to have an adult who is liked and trusted in a nearby room. The child is given permission to go to that adult whenever he or she wants to. If there is no adult available the next best alternative is to show the child the way to reception and again give him or her permission to leave the room and go to reception at any time. Experience shows that while children seem to be reassured by knowing they can leave the room they rarely do so.

It is useful to start the work of the first session by asking the child to write labels for the doors of the therapy room and of the room where the familiar adult is waiting or labels showing the way out to reception. This has a number of benefits. Firstly it emphasises to children that they can leave the room and will not get lost. A label such as 'Jane's room, please keep out' demonstrates that the therapy room is the child's territory for the duration of the session which increases the youngster's feelings of security and of being special. While the children are writing the labels their ability to use pen and paper can be assessed. Great sensitivity is needed in order not to embarrass those who cannot write well. With children who cannot write it is worth simply asking them to draw a picture of themselves and their familiar adult, the worker then adds the words. When a child can only write very slowly it may be expedient for the worker to offer to make one of the labels.

Care has to be taken to stick the labels at the appropriate height. Usually this is at the child's eye level. However, one thirteen-year-old who had been neglected and had consequently failed to grow properly was indignant when the label was placed at her eye level. 'What are you putting it there for? I'm not a child you know.'

It is important to ensure early in the first session that the children understand why they are attending and what they can expect from the worker. It is important that they are told simply but truthfully. It is worth asking them why they think they are coming. A frequent response is 'Don't know' even when it is known they have already been prepared for the session. This is often because they are rather confused about what is happening and are afraid of giving the 'wrong answer'. If it seems that a particular child knows and wants to explain but is too frightened to do so, it may be worth giving encouragement by asking questions. 'Have you been feeling sad?' The child nods. 'Do you think that coming here is something to do with feeling sad?' If a youngster shows no desire to offer an explanation he should be told in a direct way but any implication of fault on his part must be avoided – for example, not 'Because you told your teacher daddy was hitting you and making you sad' but rather 'Because we heard that your daddy was hitting you and making you sad'.

At the beginning of the first session children need time to play freely, exploring the toys. This helps them to relax and feel comfortable. It is very difficult for youngsters to see new toys and not play with them immediately. Allowing children free play will also show the worker which toys they like best. In the case of those teenagers who do not want to use toys, a general talk about their hobbies and interests serves a similar purpose, helping them to relax and become familiar with both worker and setting.

Provision of a drink and biscuits is another useful preliminary. Making a drink and finding the biscuits can be used in subsequent sessions as an opening ritual which youngsters often find reassuring. Experience shows that very often children consume neither drink nor biscuits until the end of the session but it is worth having them available during the interview.

The preliminaries having been completed, it is time to start the core work. It is often helpful to begin by asking the chidren to draw their families. Such drawings reveal a considerable amount of information about their view of themselves and their family relationships. The importance of grandparents can be ascertained by their inclusion or exclusion. The names given to various father figures can be demonstrated in those families where a mother has a number of co-habitees and vice versa. In one case a seven-year-old drew her mother as large but her brother, father,and herself as the same size. It was revealed that the father had been indulging in sexual 'games' with his children. Interpretations must however be made with extreme care, a nine-year-old who was not very adept at using pencils drew her mother as much larger than her father. This was not because the mother was more important than her father but simply because she had difficulty drawing her mother's plump shape and kept redrawing the lines until the figure became very large.

Adolescents may prefer to draw up a family-tree. This usually involves going back as far as possible in the family history. Usually youngsters can only go back to their grandparents, although often when their interest is kindled they may want to ask relatives about earlier generations. Sometimes this exercise can reveal patterns of abuse handed down from one generation to the next. It may also uncover hidden worries, for example one teenage boy commented, 'Uncle John was no good, He was sent away from home because he stole money. I've had to leave home so I guess I'm as bad.'

The helping process

There are a number of components of the helping process in relation to abused children and their siblings. These include: the expression of feelings, messages to counter misconceptions, the acquisition of new roles and strategies for self-protection.

The expression of emotions

The most important task of the therapist is to watch and listen to the children, allowing them to express both verbally and non-verbally their fears and feelings. At first sight this seems a relatively simple task but there are many factors which inhibit abused children and which will have to be overcome before they can express any strong feelings.

They may not be able to trust anyone. The worker therefore has to prove that he or she is trustworthy. Being open about what is happening will help. As the Cleveland Inquiry report (1988) recommends 'Children are entitled to a proper explanation appropriate to their age, to be told why they are being taken away from home and given some idea of what is going to happen to them.'

The therapist should be introduced by his or her name and job title not as 'aunty . . .' or 'a friend'. An experienced therapist comments:

Sometimes, with the uneasy acknowledgement of the differences in the relationship to adult and child clients, we feel that it is necessary to go under an assumed name for the benefit of the child. In this way a social worker may refer to himself not as a 'caseworker' but as a 'friend'. Unfortunately this avowal of friendship may be received cynically by the child. . . . Actually the word 'caseworker' is a nice empty package for the child who meets it for the first time, and we are in a position to fill it and give it significance by what we do and by what we are to the child. (Fraiberg, 1952, pp. 59–60)

It is worth reiterating that when recording equipment or one-way screens are being used they should be shown to the children. The youngsters have as much right as adults to raise objections and have the equipment switched off or the curtains drawn across the screen. If a child is very interested in, or upset by the camera or screen then the time spent allowing him or her to play with them may help to satisfy curiosity and allay fears.

The worker also needs to be honest in relation to the issue of confidentiality. The children can be assured that only people who are in a position to help either them or other children will be allowed to know what the child does or says in a session. Complete confidentiality cannot be guaranteed because during therapy children may indicate that they or another child was more seriously injured or mistreated than first thought; this will require the involvement of investigating agencies in response to the new allegations. The Cleveland Report again recommends, 'Professionals should not make promises which cannot be kept to the child, and in the light of possible court proceedings should not promise a child that what is said in confidence can be kept in confidence'.

In order to appreciate children's feelings and emotions they need to be helped to describe at least some aspects of their abuse. Assuming the matter has been properly investigated, there will be no need for the worker to extract precise details from the youngster. Nevertheless if the worker is to understand and help then he or she will have to share some of the child's experiences. Children might be encouraged to begin by using a dolls' house or a drawing of the home to say which rooms they disliked and where they felt safe. Dolls or modelling clay/plasticine figures representing the family may help youngsters re-enact events. They may prefer to describe what happened through a puppet or cuddly toy. Children may also be persuaded to talk down a 'no-secrets' telephone. This can simply be a disused or toy telephone decorated to look special.

The children may be inhibited by both imaginary and well-founded fears. Certain fears can be anticipated and allayed. The children need not be afraid that the worker will punish them. Children whose abuse has involved their bottoms and other private parts may worry that they will be in trouble for using 'rude words'. They can be helped by using 'anatomical dolls' or books like *A Very Touching Book* (Hindmann, 1983) which contains cartoon sketches of naked bodies.

In the therapeutic interview anatomical dolls should be kept out of sight until required and they may well not be needed. If used they should be introduced to the child carefully as special dolls which can help children who have had uncomfortable experiences. The tongue and navel can be shown and the child asked what they call these parts. When the private parts are shown the child is again invited to name them. The worker may perhaps ask 'Families often have their own names for these parts; what does your family call this?' If the child cannot name the part then the worker can give a few suggestions based on the terms in use locally 'Doctors call it a penis, but some people call it a willie, or a winkie, what would you like to call it?' Eventually youngsters will be able to build up a vocabulary for private parts with which they feel comfortable and which they know will not be condemned by the therapist.

Children may be frightened of being thought of as 'rude' not just by using certain words but by dwelling on matters concerning activities which are connected with private areas of the body. Children may also have been made to feel dirty because they wet the bed or soiled themselves. Workers can demonstrate that they accept such matters without condemnation by perhaps playing with a whoopee cushion, listening to rude jokes or by encouraging messy play. Sticky poster paints for hand and finger pictures or sand and water provide delightful sensations and can be used to show how the therapist is unperturbed by mess.

On the other hand if given too much freedom children may fear that they and the situation will run out of control. The worker has to demonstrate that the limits of the session will be maintained by for example finishing on time, insisting that the mess is eventually cleared up and being gently firm if the child's behaviour becomes unmanageable.

Guilt about what has happened may also prevent children from expressing their feelings. A non-judgemental attitude on the part of the therapist is essential. It is also important that this attitude is maintained in relation to the activities of the perpetrators described by the child. It is all right for the worker to say, 'You have the right to be angry with her' if the child shows anger against an abusive mother but not, 'I feel angry with her'. This is because the children's feelings towards their abusers may range from the intensely loyal (remember the Stockholm syndrome?) to the ambivalent. Children may feel that adults will condemn them for having positive feelings for the perpetrator.

There is a useful exercise which helps children express feelings. The worker draws three blank heads. The youngsters are then invited to fill in the faces, drawing expressions to demonstrate how the people are feeling. There is a tendency for abused children to choose sadness, happiness and anger. The therapist can join in by filling in a set of faces with feelings that the child might have such as embarrassment, fear and loneliness. When the youngster has finished the worker can ask 'What makes you angry?', 'What used to make you sad?', 'What would make you happy?'. The therapist then uses his or her own drawings to explore additional emotions.

Most abused children have some anger. This may not be directed towards the perpetrator. Often it is suppressed only to be turned against the children themselves in the form of self-denigration and depression. There are games and exercises which help children express anger safely and direct it towards those with whom they have a right to be angry. In one game the children choose a doll to represent the abuser and are then encouraged to express anger against the doll. Similarly they can model or draw a representation of the abuser then screw it up, toss it away or throw objects at it. Many children find these difficult exercises. One girl preferred to keep winding a toy turntable round and round, getting faster and rougher as she talked. Another expressed her anger by attacking the worker (who was protected by a shield) with a toy sword pretending that he represented the various members of her family with whom she was angry.

Marie, Helen and Sarah all emphasised how isolated they felt. Young clients can be helped to realise that they are not the only people who are abused. There are a number of well-known stories such as Cinderella and David Copperfield which provide examples to youngsters who are physically and emotionally abused or neglected. There are fewer stories for sexually-abused children but some videos and books have been produced on the subject which can be shared with them.

One reason for isolation is that the children have been so hurt that they have built up a protective barrier. Here a hedgehog puppet is useful. Youngsters can be shown how the hedgehog is so prickly on the outside that nobody can cuddle him when he feels in danger. But underneath he is soft and if he feels safe he can get close to people.

For some children gentle touching and cuddling is either unknown and alien or a preliminary to sexual activities. Yet people in distress can benefit from physical comfort and abused children need to feel they are not untouchable. Remember how Helen backed off from her father who wanted to cuddle her in a kindly, fatherly fashion? She felt too dirty and guilty to be touched by him. The worker can begin to give physical comfort through the use of puppets. His or her hand touches the child's hand, both safely enclosed by the puppet. Sometimes puppets are not needed as the youngster is able to accept a reassuring squeeze of the hand or shoulder.

Children are often very confused about what has happened to them. It will help if they can be encouraged to give an account of their experiences which may then be sketched out. A child who has had a lot of changes will be helped by making a life-story book. As described in Chapter 6, this is a device which has now been used to good effect with children who have spent time in care and have experienced different care-givers.

In cases of sexual abuse children's experiences can be clarified through the use of simple 'facts of life' books. A twelve-year-old girl, Emma, whose father had attempted to rape her older sister could not understand why there were restrictions on her father's activities. Emma was told, with the help of diagrams and age appropriate books, how her father's actions might have resulted in her sister having a baby by him. The girl and worker then tried to draw a family-tree including the hypothetical baby. As the girl saw how difficult it would be for the baby to sort out parents from grandparents or aunts from sisters, she began to appreciate why her father's abuse of her sister had to stop and some of her confused feelings subsided.

Workers familiar with bereavement counselling will recognise that expression of fear, guilt, anger, isolation and confusion is often associated with loss and the process of mourning. It is worth reiterating that abused children are bereaved children. They have lost security, self-esteem and unconditional love. Games and exercises that help bereaved youngsters express feelings will also be of benefit to abused ones and, of course, vice versa.

Positive messages

One feature shared by most abuse victims is that they have a low opinion of themselves. This has its roots in the belief, held by such youngsters, that if they were more worthy they would be loved by their parents. Low self-esteem is reinforced by the feelings of shame and guilt. These children need to learn that they are worth helping and spending time with. They need to be praised when praise is due.

There are a number of ways of assessing the extent of the damage to abused children's self-esteem. It can be determined by asking them whether or not they like their name. It can be useful to explore this theme further by asking if they know why they were given particular names and if they have a family nick name. Sarah's father, in his contempt for his wife and daughters, gave the two girls nick names usually given to boys.

Youngsters who do not like themselves are often reluctant to draw or model themselves. The child that can paint him or herself as large and as colourful as any other figure is likely to have a more buoyant self-esteem than youngsters who refuse to paint themselves or do so reluctantly as a tiny, faint figure or a grotesque one. Slow, gentle encouragement to create an image of themselves as attractive is one way of helping enhance their self-esteem. Older, imaginative children may like to draw themselves as trees and explain the drawing. One teenager drew herself as a stark tree with no roots or leaves but with big, black patches on the trunk. This provided an eloquent witness to her feelings of bleakness, loneliness and of being disfigured by the abuse. In later sessions she was able to add leaves, draw in roots and erase the patches. This exercise reflected her progress towards a happier self-image.

A youngster's self-confidence and esteem will also be demonstrated by his or her ability to stand in front of a mirror and smile. Children who are reluctant to do so can be encouraged to try. They can also be asked to look at the mirror at home and think how lovely they are. The worker suggesting this may be met with a degree of resistance or sarcasm from the child but it is worth persisting with this exercise.

Children invariably blame themselves for the abuse. They need to be told that they were not to blame. If they are old enough to understand analogies then these can be used to illustrate the concept of adult responsibility; examples include: (1) asking who would be to blame if an adult stole some money then bought sweets for them with the stolen cash, or (2) asking who is responsible for a crash if an adult driving a car, in which a child was a passenger, had drunk too much alcohol and could not drive safely. These illustrate that even if the child appears to enjoy or benefit from the activity he or she is not to blame. Siblings of abused children also feel guilty for not being able to stop the abuse or prevent the outcome. Again time should be spent convincing them that only adults are responsible for protecting children.

In cases where the children have managed to draw attention to the abuse they need to be told that they have done the right thing. By their disclosure they have helped to protect themselves and, quite possibly, other children. In a way they may also have assisted their parents because very few parents want to see their youngsters come to harm and ultimately they will be happier if the abuse stops. But children need to know that they are too little to stop it by themselves. It is not their fault if disclosure has led to their removal into care or the disintegration of the family.

Protective work

In any family or group members will take different roles – parent, leader, facilitator, clown. When the family or group has problems individual members are often blamed for these, so becoming scape-goat, victim, black sheep or invalid. Abused children usually have a negative role and begin to behave in a way which fulfils this. Others, like Marie, take on a parenting role comforting their mother or father and protecting siblings.

During therapy youngsters may have expressed feelings and taken on board certain messages but if they have not learnt new roles they will remain as parent or scapegoat when they join their original or new family or group. Thus before or during their involvement in family or group work they will benefit from individual therapy to help them acquire a new role.

If their role was a parental one they need to learn that responsibility lies with adults and not with children. One eight-year-old, Lisa, who had tried to protect her younger brothers and sisters, devised a game for herself. Using a farm set she put all the baby animals into an enclosure. She then chose two strong cart-horses and placed them with the baby animals. She said that it was for the adult animals to look after the babies. The worker was able to endorse this and play the game over and over again until Lisa was convinced that both she and her siblings had a right to be looked after by adults.

A child who has been the scapegoat will benefit from any exercise that enhances self-worth and teaches assertiveness. They can be encouraged to stand in front of a mirror and say, 'I am good, I am pretty' and similar postive things about themselves. They can act out, with dolls, models or puppets, stories that reflect their situation but with changed endings which ensure they are not scapegoated in the new version. They can also role-play possible situations in which they might be exploited or bullied, learning through these how to defend themselves.

Children do not deserve to be exploited or injured by their parents however they behave. Adults have a duty to guide, protect and provide for children while children have a right to demand this of adults. Children can therefore learn that although they may not be able to resist someone more powerful, they nevertheless have a right to try to protect themselves and a right to seek help from someone who is able to protect them.

One game emphasises this right and encourages youngsters to think about the people they can turn to for assistance. It involves the child cnoosing something to represent a castle of which they are sovereign. With them in the castle are all the people and things they like – their parents, ice-cream, going to the cinema, their brothers and sisters, grandma, birthdays. Outside the castle and threatening its happiness and security is an army of all the people and things they do not like – spiders, a certain teacher, ghosts, crocodiles, being hit, daddy drinking and being angry. Between the threatening army and the castle is another army of all the people who can protect them – mummy, grandma, a favourite teacher, a social worker, the police. If a child prefers animals or science fiction this theme can be adapted to a farm threatened by wild animals or a planet under attack from aliens.

In the case of children who have been sexually abused it is worth ensuring that they understand the difference between touch which is benign and that which is inappropriate. There is good touching like stroking a cuddly toy, bad touching such as being pinched and 'not good' touching which makes them feel uncomfortable and embarrassed especially when it involves their private parts. Children who are neglected need to distinguish between greed which is taking some sweets after they have had a good meal and survival which is the right to demand food if they are hungry and to complain to someone if they are not given the food. The youngster who is beaten or sworn at can be helped to separate disobedience which may deserve punishment, from simply being in the wrong place when a parent is in a bad temper. Depending on the age of the child, stories, puppet shows or questionnaires are some of the means by which these distinctions can be illustrated.

Finally, children need to learn that there are different types of secrets and some should be kept and others should not. If by keeping a secret they, or someone else, is hurt or made to feel uncomfortable then the secret should be told to someone who can help. If they fear that there will be terrible consequences from telling someone then they can be encouraged to use a trick like crossing their fingers to ward off any evil. Unfortunately, this may not help those abused children who have a realistic fear of being taken away from home or upsetting their parents but it will help in cases where the threat is unrealistic, for example where a child is told he will be turned into a frog if he discloses.

Ending individual work

The ending of individual work may signify the beginning of family therapy or group membership, although the child may have been involved in these at the same time. When the end of individual sessions means that the child will not see the worker again care has to be taken to end on a positive note. Sometimes on the last planned session children divulge information which may lead them to believe that the worker will reject them or be destroyed by the information. In these cases, as mentioned earlier, the worker needs to arrange a follow-up meeting to demonstrate to the children that they have not been rejected nor has the worker been harmed by anything they might have said. This follow-up can be informal such as spending a few minutes with the youngster before an access visit.

If the planned sessions are to be few then the child can be told at the outset that they will see the worker for, perhaps, six meetings. After each meeting the child can be reminded that they have five or however many meetings left. If the number of sessions has been left open then, as the worker feels termination is drawing near, the child should be prepared for the fact that he or she will be moving on to a new stage.

Most youngsters enjoy individual work despite the fact that sessions can be painful for them. Sometimes they become attached to a certain toy, but it is rarely possible for them to keep it. However, they can be given a photograph of their favourite toy. Most children accept the fact that play equipment has to stay where it belongs. This can lead to a useful discussion of what home is and why, in the case of a child in care, people have to leave home. Children can also become fond of their therapist; again they can be given a photograph or some other memento such as a badge, button or a drawing. Workers may wish to draw a picture of a trophy and give it to the child as a prize for being brave. This exchange is particularly useful if the worker has asked to keep some of the child's drawings.

Finally, individual therapy may help victims cope for a while but sometimes they need assistance again later in life when they reach another significant point such as the birth of their own baby. Such events can awaken long-buried memories and emotions. Children can be prepared for this by being told that occasionally people have problems which re-occur but they have the right to demand support again.

4

Work with Children in the Family Context

As defined in the introduction, child abuse occurs in the family context and therefore it would seem logical that helping the child should, in many cases, take place within the family context. This chapter is not designed as an in-depth study of family therapy. It looks at the type of help which a social worker, with some understanding of family dynamics, can undertake. All the suggestions are based on practical experience. The workers who used the methods described were all busy professionals with many other demands on their time and with few facilities. They did not regard themselves as 'experts' but they acquired an expertise by careful planning, by accepting guidance from colleagues, by practising techniques and by always being sensitive to the feelings and needs of the clients.

One concept underlying this chapter is that of the family as a system. A system is made up of sub-systems and is influenced by other external systems. A family is affected by the nature and activities of its members – i.e. its sub-systems, and by external systems such as its local community, neighbours and official bodies. The family system refers not just to the nuclear family but to other members of the household and to important relatives and acquaintances who, while not living in the same house, play a major part in the family activities. A family is called 'functional' when it is providing a safe, nurturing environment in which the children can develop appropriately. When the family system endangers the life and well-being of its members it is termed 'dysfunctional'.

This concept is applicable to all families not just those in which abuse occurs. Similarly the suggestions in this chapter can be adapted to help with many different situations in which there is some form of family distress.

Advantages and disadvantages

Advantages

One advantage of family work is that it can bring to the fore long-buried flames of affection. As explained in the first chapter, children can become attached to abusing parents. There is a process which manifests itself in something akin to the Stockholm syndrome. The youngsters often want the abuse to stop but crave the abuser's love. In many cases abusive parents have a substantial degree of affection for their offspring, despite abusing them. The faintest ember of love in the parents is worth fanning, it may burst into flame, inspiring them to adopt more caring attitudes and behaviour.

Another advantage is that family work can transform a dysfunctional family into a functional one. This is in the child's best interests because youngsters have a strong need to belong to a family. This feeling is reinforced by the emphasis on the family in advertising, in school, on television, in magazines and comics. Promotions of a wide variety of goods from soup to saloon cars so often show a happy family group of father, mother and two or three cheerful children.

A further advantage of family work is that, because the family is a system, if there is change in one member, the system as a whole will be changed. It will attempt to shift simply to maintain the status quo. However, if the family is committed to change and is being helped in this endeavour then its functioning will be improved. During a family session a father who has accepted his responsibility for the abuse can be helped to apologise to the children. This results in the children being relieved of guilt and responsibility. They also learn through their father's example that if they do wrong they should admit the fact. This marks the beginning of a new, honest, open form of family communication.

Where the children are to remain at home or return to their family it is futile at best and dangerous at worst to work with only one or two family members. Abused children learn to adapt to the abuse. Their behaviour may seem to be abnormal but when seen in the family context it is a normal adjustment to an abnormal situation. Jessica Cameronchild was physically and emotionally abused from her earliest years. As a teenager she attempted suicide; one of her brothers had already killed himself. Jessica was hospitalised and given intensive therapy. She wrote:

> The psychiatrist and hospital staff were, in fact, setting up a very futile and destructive double bind by putting me on a program that required me to give up defenses which were vital to my survival at home . . . the course of

my treatment exacerbated the violence for my brothers at home, condoned our parents' past mistreatment of us, reinforced their denial, and augmented my futile view of the world in general. (Cameronchild, 1978, p. 148)

Treating the parents without involving the children is equally fraught with danger. The aim of any treatment is change; with abusive parents it is likely to be directed towards a change in behaviour in relation to the children. This is usually a long, slow process. If the youngsters are living at home the abuse is unlikely to stop straight away. Meanwhile, although the parents are gaining insights and trying to change, some abusive behaviour will continue, with all that that implies in terms of the children's development. If the children are directly involved in the process than at least they are receiving some assistance to balance the negative effects of the continuing abuse.

The children themselves will have adapted to the parents' abusive behaviour; Marie talked about learning to stay one step ahead of her father. When the parents alone are given therapy they will change but the youngsters may become confused and more frightened. They were secure with the 'devil' they knew. Now they are insecure as they can no longer anticipate parental behaviour. Where a youngster had the role of victim or scapegoat it might not be needed as parental functioning improves. But this may mean the child no longer feels of value to the parents and the fear of being killed by them re-emerges. Children may react by trying to provoke the parent into abusing them again in order to restore the former, familiar situation.

Patterns and forms of communication are important in families. Parents given help will learn to communicate more openly and directly with the children. But if the youngsters have not learnt the same patterns of communication they will again become confused. In one family the eldest daughter had protected her younger siblings. She had always acted as their spokeswoman, bearing the brunt of her father's anger and violence. The parents tried relating more directly to the younger children, who did not understand what was happening and became frightened and unresponsive. The eldest girl felt ignored and rejected. The parents became frustrated as their new behaviour, instead of making the situation better, seemed to make it worse. Family work which teaches all members to learn new patterns of communication together would have avoided these difficulties.

There is an advantage in family work even when there are no plans to return the children. As already noted abusive parents are important to their offspring, as is a sense of belonging. It will be recalled that although Sarah disliked her father and the abuse, she did not have a feeling of joyful liberation when she was sent away from home to boarding school. She simply felt abandoned, devoid of a sense of belonging. There is merit in forging positive links between family members, so that they remain united in spirit, even when they do not live together. The exception to this would be those few cases in which the children are to be placed with permanent substitute carers and all contact with the family of origin is to be curtailed.

Without family work access visits can be acrimonious. The child who disclosed may be blamed for the separation of family members. This may pervade the extended family with perhaps grandparents and other relatives sending birthday presents to all the children except the one who disclosed. Family work can result in all members understanding and acknowledging that the parents are responsible for the abuse and its consequences, the children are relieved of feelings of guilt and shame, while whatever love there is in the family is expressed and shared.

Disadvantages

For the majority of people the familiar is comfortable, the unknown is usually feared. Change often means moving from the familiar to the unknown. Slow evolution is relatively comfortable and achieves a balance between the discomfort of change and the need to adapt to changing circumstances. A sudden crisis may cause a sudden change but without any other intervention the system will re-create the situation which existed before the crisis.

Disclosure or professional intervention in an abusing family is a crisis. The family may change temporarily but once the crisis has passed the family will try to revert to the former situation. In cases of sexual abuse one parent may bar the abusing partner from the home at first, only to have him or her back once the case conference or legal proceedings have been completed. A lone social worker is unlikely to be able to resist this powerful process inherent in all systems of returning to the status quo – called 'homeostatis'.

The main problem encountered by a therapist attempting to intervene single-handed is the possibility of being absorbed into the family system. Families are adept at finding roles for people who could be a threat. Roles include 'rich uncle' – the constant provider of material goods, 'family friend' – the confidant who can be trusted to keep family secrets or 'fairy god-mother' – the person who will solve all problems instantly by magic. In some cases the worker may become clearly allied with the abusing parent, condemning the children's behaviour as provocative or seductive. Because the needs and demands of its members often conflict a single professional trying to meet the requirements of the whole family is faced with an impossible task. He or she is likely to become emotionally exhausted or will only find sufficient energy to spare for just one or two members.

Joint family work

The advantages of family work appear to outweigh the disadvantages. The main drawback is that the worker may become part of the dysfunctional family system. There are however a number of strategies which can prevent this. Most require some form of joint work, i.e. professionals working closely together to achieve the same objective. This is not the same as interdisciplinary co-operation; a family doctor and an education welfare officer (EWO) can work in close co-operation but the primary aim of the doctor is the good health of the family whereas that of EWO is the proper education of the children.

Various models for joint working will be suggested in this chapter but it is acknowledged that sometimes local resources are such that there is only one therapist available for the whole family. In these circumstances other agencies such as the school and primary medical team have a duty to help the family worker by monitoring the situation as far as possible and passing on relevant information. Too often such agencies expect the worker to seek information from them instead of volunteering potentially important details.

Practitioners who are having to work on their own should also have a supervisor able to provide an objective view of the family and of their involvement, thereby helping to guard against over-identification with part of the family and emotional exhaustion. In instances where the supervisor has insufficient knowledge of both family work and child abuse the worker should be encouraged to seek the advice of a consultant. The supervisor and consultant will then liaise in order to ensure that their approaches are consistent and are not presenting the worker with further conflicts.

Co-working

Working with a co-therapist is a tried and tested approach to both group and family work and offers considerable advantages to worker and family alike. Two workers are more able to resist the pressure of the family system. It is more difficult for a family to find roles for two new members than it is to absorb just one new addition.

The needs of all the different members of the family can never be met by just one worker. Even where there is a single mother with one infant it is often difficult to give attention to both. A mother who is abusing her baby is likely to be under great stress and make considerable emotional demands. She is unlikely to tolerate the worker spending a lot of time relating to the baby because she needs the attention for herself. Yet the baby will also be distressed by the abuse he or she has suffered and by the mother's tension. The therapist needs to build up a relationship with the infant, becoming a familiar figure for the baby who will then accept handling or examination by the worker should this become necessary. Small children have died because social workers have paid a lot of attention to the parents and too little to the children.

A useful role-play exercise illustrates the problems inherent in the one therapist for one family approach. Participants represent a family consisting of a single distressed parent with two children who are being negleced plus a lone social worker visiting the home in order to alleviate the family problems. Invariably participants report that the visit made matters worse, especially for those playing the parts of the children. If the worker gives most of his or her attention to the parent, the children feel doubly neglected. However, if the worker spends time with the children the parent feels his or her needs are being ignored or treated too lightly and thereby experiences more distress. He or she may fear that the worker is only looking for evidence in order to remove the children.

This situation is helped if two therapists are involved, one attending to the needs of certain family members while the other concentrates on the remaining members. Often the split is between the parents and children or between the males and females in the family. Sometimes the needs of one person are so overwhelming that one worker concentrates all efforts on that person leaving his or her colleagues to attend to all other demands.

Co-working especially where one worker is male and the other female can provide a model of adult co-operation and open communication for the parents. The two workers can demonstrate to both parents and children that mutual respect and joint decision-making between men and women is possible. A further incidental benefit is, that in potentially violent situations, being accompanied by a colleague can offer some protection.

The drawbacks of this way of working are self-evident. Both therapists must be competent and confident. A defensive co-worker who becomes possessive of the clients and keeps trying to 'score points' over his or her colleague is a destructive force. Two workers can start to mirror the split in the family; identifying with different factions, thereby reinforcing the family's dysfunction. The abused children may not only be criticised and scapegoated by siblings and parents but also by two workers. One worker absorbed into the family system is bad, two workers so absorbed is more than twice as bad.

In hard-pressed social work agencies there may not be sufficient staff to allow for co-working. One solution is to link up with another agency such as probation, education or health departments. However, probation officers, community teachers and health visitors may well have different objectives, constraints and priorities which make any commitment to long-term co-work impossible.

A further problem is that of supervision. Co-workers even from the same agency may have different supervisors. There are a number of solutions: one supervisor may agree to have a prime role, while the second simply retains an overview in order to satisfy the demands of accountability; alternatively there may be periodical four-way supervision sessions; a third alternative is the appointment of a totally independent supervisor just for a particular case.

Where the therapists have the same supervisor there are still problems about whether they are seen individually or together. The best solution seems to be to have individual sessions, with arrangements made for the co-worker to be available for part of the time. Another solution is to alternate individual and joint sessions.

Recording and case accountability also present problems. If the therapists are from different agencies they will keep individual records but if they are from the same agency then only one is needed. Alternate recording of sessions evens out the workload but can cause confusion. The most practical solution appears to be for one worker to have prime responsibility for recording, booking facilities, liaison with other agencies and all other aspects of case management.

Live supervision

As its name implies – like a live audience for a television show – supervisors are present during the family session. They are more than mere observers; their task requires active participation. Live supervision can take a variety of forms depending on the facilities available. In its simplest form one supervisor sits quietly, taking notes in a corner of the same room as the therapists. At the other extreme a large group of colleagues can view one or two workers through a one-way screen or video monitor link. In a session which appeared to be effective, one worker interviewed the family while two live supervisors sat in the same room taking notes and operating a video camera, the recording was later shown to a case consultant. It is perhaps remarkable how both therapists and family members can put cameras, screens and additional people to the back of their minds and concentrate on the task in hand.

An important principle is that all family members should agree to the involvement of the live supervisors. They should understand what is happening and accept that there will be interventions. It is made clear that the supervisor is there to assist the worker who in consequence will be able to help the family more effectively. The family is usually introduced to all the supervisors, although if there is a big group watching through a screen or monitor it is probably most appropriate to introduce a representative of the group while inviting the family members to meet the rest after the session.

There are planned breaks during the session, when supervisors and therapists can reflect on events so far and when changes in direction may be suggested. In addition there will be *ad hoc* interventions by the supervisors if the workers and family members seem to be stuck or unnecessarily avoiding important issues. These interventions can be conveyed by telephone or through ear-phones or perhaps by a knock on the door. Notes for the session and for case files are usually made by one of the supervisors, thereby leaving the therapists free to focus all their energy on the direct work with the family.

This model can prevent therapists from becoming part of the family system. For example in one case a single male worker was helping a family which appeared to be comprised of a domineering mother, a rather ineffectual father, a teenage son, Martin and three younger children. The supervisors were able to observe how the worker was being made to take over the role of forceful father in relation to Martin instead of enabling all family members to express themselves and adopt more appropriate roles.

Live supervisors can also ensure that the therapists do not focus on the needs of certain family members to the exclusion of others. An example to illustrate this is the B family. The eldest girl, Clare had been sexually abused by her father. The mother was distressed when she discovered what was happening and she was also concerned about the health of her only son. Mr B was upset by the disclosure and its consequences to his career. During one session the supervisors observed how the two workers were focusing attention on the parents and were failing to see Clare's anger and distress, which was such that the supervisors entertained the possibility that she might attempt suicide. The attention of both therapists had been diverted away from Clare by the more vocal distress of the rest of the family.

There are problems inherent in live supervision, including the threat posed to therapists by the presence of colleagues who are observing and analysing their work. Related to this is the fear that they may lose credibility in the family's eyes because they seem to be frequently 'corrected' by other people. But experience shows that workers who have supervisors in whom they trust find live supervision reassuring. Once it becomes an established practice in a team, members can come to depend on it to the extent that an unsupervised session can be unnerving. A family can be helped to appreciate this method of working by the explanation that it is important that it receives the best help possible and that two or more heads are better than one.

Another problem is that of the time and commitment required of more than one worker. However it is better in the long run to have effective therapy which achieves real and positive change in family functioning rather than one worker intervening to stave off yet another crisis for a while. There is little point in intervention which does not give effective help to abused children and merely contributes to the process of learned helplessness. Live supervision has a further advantage as it is a little more flexible than co-working because the supervisor does not have to be the same person each time. It is important to clarify that live supervision and co-working can be combined with co-therapists being live supervised.

It is perhaps worth highlighting the fact that live supervision is not used exclusively in family work. It can be used with groups, pairs and individuals. However, it is especially valuable, as has already been noted, as a protection against the therapists becoming absorbed into a very powerful but ultimately destructive family system. It is particularly useful, as the case of Clare illustrated, in ensuring that the needs of the children are not overlooked.

Case manager model

It has been shown that different family members have differing therapeutic requirements, yet it is difficult for one or even two workers to give effective help to each family member. The danger is that the needs of the quietest, most withdrawn person will be overlooked, yet he or she may be the most distressed individual who could, in silent despair, attempt suicide. Alternatively the needs of the youngest member, especially one not yet able to verbalise feelings coherently will be ignored. A total team approach therefore has much to commend it.

Often a team consists of professionals from different agencies. One such team was comprised of a probation officer, a social worker from the local social services department (SSD) and one from a voluntary agency (VA). The team was involved with the C family. The eldest children Jane, Brian and Bruce had been physically abused and Jane had also been sexually abused by the father. Two younger daughters, Elaine and Emma, had probably not been abused. Mr C was convicted of the sexual offences and placed on probation. Jane chose to come into care. The probation officer worked with Mr C and undertook some marital counselling with Mr and Mrs C. The SSD social worker gave Mrs C some practical help when for a period Mr C left home, helped with the care arrangements for Jane and focused his remaining time and energy on the emotional needs of Mrs C and the boys. The VA worker concentrated on therapy for Jane and protective work with the younger girls. The team could well have started to mirror the conflicts between individuals and sub-groups in the family, creating more confusion than already existed. Despite the abundance of helpers intervention could have been ineffective and the needs of some members ignored.

In order to avoid the obvious pitfalls a case manager was appointed. She had no direct involvement in the family but had a vital role in co-ordinating the intervention of the individual workers. The case manager was responsible for organising meetings of the three workers at acceptable intervals. Fortnightly or monthly meetings seemed to be appropriate, depending on the stage of the case. During meetings the therapists would outline their involvement since the previous meeting and report on the situation of the family members to whom they were committed. The case manager then helped them to reflect on what was happening and plan for the next stage of the work. During one meeting there was open conflict between the probation officer and Jane's therapist. The case manager was able to help the workers see how they were reflecting the anger and tension that had been mounting between Mr C and Jane. She was also responsible for keeping a record of the meeting and arranging the date and venue of the next.

This model is appropriate when the family is in considerable conflict and where work needs to be undertaken with individuals and dyads before total family therapy sessions are a feasible option. There were meetings between Mr and Mrs C conducted by the probation officer sometimes on his own and sometimes with the SSD worker. There were interviews held between Mrs C and Jane with the VA and SSD workers, who were also present at meetings between Jane and her brothers. When eventually they whole family met in session the SSD worker was the therapist with the probation officer and VA worker acting as live supervisors, helping to ensure that no family member was ignored or scapegoated. This session was recorded on video and the case manager was able to view it later.

The case management model can be used with comparatively small families. In a case where a mother was neglecting her two small children a case manager co-ordinated the efforts of a play therapist for the children, of a health visitor, of a family aide and of a social worker who had access to resources for the family. The model can also be used with a large team. In another case Ricky, a teenage boy, sexually abused his young sister. A residential worker helped Ricky who was received into care, a play therapist helped the little girl and two Child and Family Guidance Unit workers provided marital and family therapy. Because there were several other children in the family a local authority social worker helped with practical arrangements and gave attention to the other youngsters still at home. The individual and joint interventions of the various helpers were co-ordinated by a case manager.

When this model is used the family have to be kept informed of what is happening and are made aware of the involvement and function of the case manager although he or she does not usually meet the family. If the family ask to meet the manager this should be arranged towards the end of the intervention.

The main objection to this model is that it appears to be costly. However, each worker can be involved in several of these cases concurrently because the emotional demands are spread between a number of different professionals. One worker trying to achieve the same objective on his or her own would have found the task overwhelming and time consuming. Instead of spending several hours each week contacting fellow workers by telephone, efforts are co-ordinated by a fortnightly or monthly two-hour session with only brief practical telephone calls in between when necessary.

Supervision is another problem. The effectiveness of the model does not seem to decline if the case manager is also the supervisor of one of the workers. However it is adversely affected if the supervisor of any therapist feels threatened by the case manager's influence. It is inappropriate for agency supervisors to attend case management meetings. Their presence would make the sessions too large and unwieldy. Nevertheless, occasional additional meetings can be arranged which supervisors attend, at which they can give voice to their concerns.

A final problem which may affect team functioning is that of hidden agendas. One reason for these may be that one or more of the workers were themselves abused as children and their professional functioning is impaired because they have not yet resolved this background problem. When a case manager suspects that there may be a personal issue involved – because a therapist is perhaps over-identifying with a family member – he or she should arrange for an individual discussion with the worker to sort out a way of helping other team members appreciate what is happening.

Family centres

Joint working is a characteristic of family centres. There are many different projects which are called family centres but this section refers to one particular model which provides intensive help for abusing families.

The model involves the total family attending a centre on several days a week. The objective is to help family relationships, provide play and structure for the children and training in parentcraft for the parents. Very often physical abuse and neglect occur because the parents do not know how to care for their children and become overwhelmed by the situation. Usually these parents are loving and caring but had a poor example of parenting in their own childhood. At family centres the parents are taught practical skills such as how to cook nutritional meals, budget family finances, maintain hygiene and establish a routine. In relationship to their children they learn about normal development in order that they do not have unrealistic expectations of the youngsters and are helped to appreciate their children's needs for stimulation and security. Because of the high staff-to-family ratio special programmes can be tailored to meet the particular requirements of each family.

These tasks place strenuous demands on the team of centre staff, who liaise closely with the family's own social worker. A satisfactory staff ratio is approximately three workers to five or six families. Six months attendance at the centre is usually required, as is a commitment by the family to attend. Although attendance is commonly on a daily basis there are some residential centres. These provide a more intensive experience for the family which can be very beneficial, but they are costly to run. The co-operation of housing authorities is also required if the family does not own its home and is to vacate if for several months.

Facilitating communications

In family work it is important that all family members take part. This means that people beyond the nuclear family may have to be included if they are an important part of the family system. A common example is that of the grandparent who frequently looks after the children and has tried to protect them. It also means that all members who are present at a session need to participate actively. It is easy for the more assertive family members to dominate the session, while the youngest or quietest are virtually ignored. There are a number of techniques which ensure that everyone present is included.

Verbal techniques

One way of including all family members in the verbal component of the session is by using circular questioning. One member is asked how another member reacts or would react in a given situation. The accuracy of the answer is checked with the second member. For example instead of asking the father what he does when the children arrive home late after school, the youngest child could be asked, 'What does dad do when you come home late?' The child may say, 'He gets angry'. The father is then asked, 'Do you get angry?' The father might explain, 'Yes, because I'm worried about them when they are late'. When one family member is very quiet another can be asked on that member's behalf. An apparently sullen teenage girl, Mandy, who had been physically and sexually abused by her step-father understandably refused to say anything during the first few family sessions. The workers therefore, having in vain already asked Mandy directly, asked another family member 'What would Mandy reply to that question if she was able to do so?' She was then asked if the response was accurate. She only had to nod or shake her head. Although she could not talk she was able to voice her opinions through other family members.

Care has to be taken in this form of questioning. Asking about the feelings of others poses difficulties for family members. The question, 'How does mum feel when you do that?' posed to a cynical adolescent may well be met with the response, 'Dunno, why don't you ask her yourself?' It is marginally better to ask, 'How do you think mum feels?' thereby inquiring about his opinion rather than directly about anothers feelings. When the response, 'Dunno' is still forthcoming it is important not to make the youngster feel that he is being condemned by the worker; so instead of irritably saying, 'But I'm asking you, not her' the most appropriate response might be a move to a new area of questioning after a comment such as, 'I guess it's not easy to talk about how someone else feels'.

Members can also be encouraged to ask each other questions. The therapist might say, 'Tommy can you ask mummy what she would like to happen?' Tommy may refuse. The mother is then invited to ask Tommy why he does not want to ask her. Yet again care has to be taken especially with children to guard against making them feel at fault if, because of shyness or anger, they cannot participate.

In some families it is evident that there is some love but this is rarely expressed and the emphasis is on bad behaviour and punishment. One useful exercise is to ask each family member in turn to say something they like about a chosen member. Then the spotlight moves on to the next person, so that each family member has heard something nice said about themselves by every other member. The therapist usually takes a turn in saying something positive about each family member but it is not necessary for the worker to be in the spotlight unless the family makes a specific request to that effect.

Non-verbal communication

One way in which the therapist can influence family dynamics is by changing the seating plan. This is obviously easier to do in a designated interview room rather than in the family's home. In one case where the daughter had taken over her mother's responsibility for her family, father and daughter used to sit together, while the mother and young son sat together leaving chairs in between each dyad for the workers. After a few sessions the workers insisted on the mother and father sitting together with the two children together. One aim of the work with the family was to distinguish between adults who were the parents and children who should be free of parental responsibility. The change in places provided a tangible demonstration of this. When a family member who should have been included in the session is absent, he or she should be seen to be included in the session by being designated an empty chair.

Family members can be asked to communicate non-verbally with other members. For example a youngster may start crying and the mother, if she does not do so spontaneously, might be invited to put her arm round the child. Again care has to be taken because if the mother refused point blank to do so the youngster might feel all the more rejected and distressed.

Exercises, role-play and video

There is a useful exercise which helps to illustrate the different perspectives of the family. Members in turn are invited to draw either themselves or the family member they consider to be most important first. This can be on a blackboard or a large sheet of paper. They then draw all the other members positioned on the paper near to or distant from each other depending on how the person drawing sees the family relationships. With a large family it is probably less time consuming to represent its members as a large dot. If this exercise has been used with Sarah's family, the two sisters may have seen how they both believed that the other sister was closest to their father, thereby dissipating some of the jealousy and misconceptions that they had about each other. Furthermore, the father would no longer have been able to play the 'your sister is better than you' game. He would have had to have drawn each child at an equal distance from him or have specified a favourite.

Mandy, mentioned earlier in this section, refused to join in this exercise. The workers accepted her reluctance. They said that, although they would like her to take part because her opinion was as valid as that of the others, she was perhaps not ready to do so. Later when everyone else had had a chance to sketch the family Mandy was again approached with the suggestion that she could tell another member or a worker where to put the family figures on her behalf. She agreed and chose her brother to act as scribe. Soon she was so involved that when her brother did not put the figures in exactly the right place she went over to the flip-chart and started drawing the family constellation herself. Coffee cups, buttons, coloured cardboard pieces or little play figures can be used instead of sketches.

Role-play is useful in helping family members rehearse what they would like to do in a given situation. An example may be of a girl who wets her bed, tries to hide the sheets, is teased by her siblings and punished by her parents. The family can practise a more constructive response – with perhaps the girl telling her mother and offering to help wash and change the sheets, while the rest of the family shows a calmer more understanding reaction.

In the case of the D family role-play was used in a slightly different way. The family was being helped through the case management model described earlier in this chapter. The daughter, Zoe had been sexually abused by her step-father. She was ambivalent about meeting him. She was frightened about being so angry that she would lose control when she met him and either attack him or dissolve into tears. Similarly Mr D was worried about his response when he met his step-daughter again for the first time since disclosure, yet he wanted to apologise to her and tell her that she was not to blame. There was a female worker supporting Zoe and a male probation officer support-ing Mr D. Eventually the workers decided that Zoe could usefully rehearse what she would like to say to her step-father by meeting the probation officer who would represent Mr D. Conversely, Mr D met the female social worker to rehearse with her his apology to Zoe.

Video can also be used in a similar way. After the completion of the various role-play meetings, Zoe still felt unable to meet her step-father, yet he was keen to apologise and she needed to hear him accept responsibility if she was ever to appreciate that she was not in some way to blame. A video recording was made of Mr D saying he was sorry, assuring Zoe that all that had happened was his fault and showing concern for her welfare. Zoe agreed to see the video and was supported by her therapist as she watched it. She was able to see her step-father's sincerity and was given further important evidence that she was not responsible for the abuse or the consequences of disclosure.

Finally, therapists can set tasks to be completed by the family between sessions. For example, a very isolated family may be encouraged to invite one of the children's friends for tea one evening before the next session. If the family does not manage this one week they can be encouraged to try again. If they still do not manage then the workers accept responsibility for setting a task which was too difficult thereby avoiding giving the family any sense of failure. It is important however not to condone the family doing more than was asked, for example inviting three friends for tea when they were only asked to invite one. Sometimes doing too much reflects over-high expectations on the part of the family, when the therapists are trying to instill a sense of reality into the situation. Furthermore some families are so sure that they will fail that they attempt more than they can manage in order to ensure their eventual failure.

One slightly paradoxical task, which is designed to succeed through failure but which usually brings some humour into the situation, is to ask the family to behave in a specific undesirable way but only under certain conditions. An example in a case of marital violence is to tell the parents that they must have an argument but it must be at 9 p.m. precisely on Monday evening when all the children are in bed and it must take place in the kitchen. Usually couples find it difficult to argue to order but this exercise helps them to start thinking about the nature of their rows and how, when and why they occur.

5

Group Work with Abused Children

Group work is a tried and tested method of enhancing the ability of people to function in a variety of settings. It has been used in recent years to help sexually abused children. Often such youngsters are offered a place in a group before they show any symptoms of distress. An assumption is made that children who have been subjected to sexual abuse have had a potentially damaging experience which warrants intervention.

Group therapy is less readily used as a method of helping physically or emotionally abused and neglected children. It seems that, unlike the victims of sexual abuse, they are only offered therapeutic help when
they display behavioural signs of disturbance. They may be involved in intermediate treatment groups if they show a tendency toward delinquency. They may be referred to a remedial group if they have problems with learning in school. They may be offered a place in a group run by a child psychotherapist if their behaviour is deemed 'difficult' or bizarre. There seem however to be few therapeutic groups for physically abused and neglected children who appear to be unaffected by their experiences. Nevertheless, although the emotional difficulties encountered by children subjected to different forms of abuse may differ in certain aspects, all abused children have many negative feelings in common. If sexually abused children benefit from group work then youngsters subjected to other forms of abuse may also benefit from group work – not because their behaviour is disturbed but simply by virtue of the fact that they have been abused.

It is worth emphasising that this does not mean that children who have been subjected to different forms of abuse would benefit from being together in the same group. Members need to have enough in common to appreciate each other's experiences. Furthermore in a mixed group the range of areas to be dealt with can become too broad for the group to be effective. Youngsters who have been emotionally and physically neglected may have no problems over secrecy but may have to learn about sharing and caring, whereas sexually abused children will need to exchange ideas about appropriate touching, sexual behaviour, the keeping of secrets and ways they can be protected from adult advances.

The value of group work

There are a number of benefits and pitfalls associated with group work. Features associated with all groups are well documented in a number of standard works (Bion, 1961; Konopka, 1972). This chapter will concentrate on those aspects of group work of particular relevance to work with abused children.

The benefits

Marie, Helen and Sarah in the second chapter all recalled a pervading feeling of isolation. Often abused children feel they are the only ones to have experienced such treatment at the hands of those who are meant to love them. Even when they are not directly mistreated but witness siblings being abused they still feel that they are the only ones with those dark feelings of anger, guilt or despair. Inevitably abused children feel that there is something abnormal or objectionable about themselves. By getting to know other children who have suffered similar experiences they learn that others share their feelings. Helen recalled that when she was about eleven she found out that a number of her friends had night-time terrors about bogey-men or monsters. As she realised that her friends' fears were unfounded she recognised that her own belief that a man with a gun was coming into her room was equally unfounded. Had she been able to share this fear earlier with her peers she might never have needed her brother's nightly visits.

Participants may find themselves admiring a fellow group member. A nine-year-old felt that another girl in her group was very pretty. Through this she learnt that abuse does not necessarily make a child unattractive. Slowly she began to acknowledge that she too had some lovely features. Role-play between young companions is more comfortable than it is when an adult has to take on the role of perpetrator. Sexually abused children in particular may become alarmed by an adult making a sexual advance, even in the context of role-play, children however can mimic adults without causing alarm to each other. A further advantage of group work is that the children may feel that they are in a 'safer' environment than they are in individual therapy alone with an adult. This, especially for sexually abused children, avoids recreating the abusive scenario.

Participants who have learnt new roles in individual therapy can practise these in the group. If, for example, they have always been a scapegoat they can try out new ways of ensuring that they do not take the blame for anything that goes wrong in the group. They may need the help of the leaders to achieve this.

Humour is more likely to occur in a group setting than it is in individual or family work. Laughter is a good tonic and it can help youngsters to come to terms with negative experiences. Marie pointed to humour when asked what helped her survive her experiences. She explained that after incidents such as the destruction of the Christmas presents, her mother and siblings were able to laugh about their father's behaviour; this made the incident more bearable as he was reduced to the status of a clown rather than that of an ogre.

Groups provide a means whereby positive messages are reinforced. This is particularly true for adolescents who are often influenced more by their peers than by adults. A teenage boy, told he is not to blame for the abuse by a therapist, may take the attitude, 'You're paid to say that'. He might, however, be more easily convinced by a group of fellow adolescents all giving him the same message.

Problems and pitfalls

The main problem for hard-pressed social workers hoping to establish a group is one of resources. Group work with children, as with adults, requires commitment by at least two therapists. They need to set aside time at regular intervals for the group sessions, as well as additional time for preparation and planning, review and recording. The same room should be used on each occasion but in many buildings meeting rooms large enough for groups are at a premium. Unless other colleagues recognise the importance of the group the workers may find that time and again their room is commandeered for a case conference or a training session.

Transport is sometimes a problem. In order to find enough children who have sufficient in common to make a viable group, members have to be drawn from a fairly wide geographical area. Children cannot be expected to make their own way to meetings, yet sometimes their caretakers' ambivalence about the group means that they prove unreliable when it comes to bringing the children for sessions. It is however unsatisfactory if the group workers have to ferry the members themselves because they need to be free to devote all their time and energy to running the session itself.

All participants have to be capable of handling the group situation.

A youngster must be able to relate to other children and share the leaders with others. They should also have begun to adopt new roles if their previous one in family and group situations was negative. Meanwhile the group leaders have to be capable of working with a number of children at once. They require skills in both direct work with abused youngsters and in group therapy and above all they need to be emotionally resilient. Commenting on her experiences of running groups for small children Eileen Vizard writes, 'From the therapist's point of view, however, a lot of experience in doing this work does not protect one against a feeling of sickness when, for instance, as happened to myself and a new co-therapist recently a 4-year-old girl turned to us in the middle of pinning on her name badge and said simply "I was raped" (Vizard, 1987, p. 19). The same author went on to note 'In theory, many mental health professionals might be able to run such groups. . . . However, in practice we know that it takes more skill, and considerably more supervision, than we had originally thought' (Vizard, 1987, p. 21).

One problem encountered when running children's groups is that their caregivers are often very concerned about what is happening in the group and may put the youngster under pressure to give details or, suspicious of what is happening, may attempt to persuade the child not to attend. Under such circumstances it is probably advisable to provide the carer with sketchy details, thereby satisfying curiosity without breaching the child's confidences.

A major pitfall is the assumption that all problems can be helped through group work. This is not the case. A prime example is that of people suffering from eating disorders. Groups help people trying to lose weight, because the element of competition is a spur to greater efforts. Unfortunately, the same process works in exactly the same way with people suffering from anorexia nervosa. Members will secretly compete to see who can lose the most weight. Anorexia nervosa is thought to be linked in some cases to sexual abuse (Oppenheimer, 1985). The idea of a group for teenage girls, who not only have the experience of sexual abuse in common but also share the problem of anorexia nervosa, is an inviting one. But, unless the group is run by someone with consummate skills, it is more likely to compound the problem of weight loss rather than help it.

Variations on the theme of group work

In many areas the number of abused children referred to the authorities remains high compared to ten or twenty years ago. Despite this there are often too few youngsters with enough in common in one area to form a viable group. Furthermore, the problems already outlined may prove too daunting for professionals who might otherwise have used group therapy. There are two methods of intervention which provide many of the advantages of group work yet avoid some of the main problems. These are 'pairing' and 'family groups'.

Pairing

As its name implies 'pairing' refers to work with two children, who are not siblings but have much in common. Usually the youngsters will have already had some individual help. They reach a stage where they need to know for certain that other children are abused and they are not alone in this respect. They may need to act out their experiences and practise strategies both for avoiding the victim role and for asserting their right to be safe and properly cared for. (To avoid confusion the pair of children with their workers will be referred to as a 'group' in this section.)

An abused youngster is invited to meet another child who has had similar experiences to him or herself. If one declines the invitation he or she is evidently not ready to cope with the situation and should not be pressurised into doing so. If both agree the group can go ahead. Where the same person has provided individual work for both children he or she will probably continue as the group therapist. In cases where each young client has had a different worker a new therapist can be designated for the group work or, alternatively, the two original workers can become joint leaders.

Once the children are introduced and feel comfortable they can be invited to draw up rules for the group. In individual work they may have each had different limits and expectations of themselves and the worker. For example one child may have been used to entering and leaving the interview room at will whereas the other child may have felt it important to ask the worker's permission. One group of two girls aged seven and nine plus one adult devised and wrote out a list which (with no apologies for the poor spelling) reads:

> Rools of the group
> no swaring
> only leave the room if ask
> no smoking
> no breking toys
> no hiting
> no secrets

The last point about 'no secrets' required much discussion. The members had to draw a distinction between being honest with each other and yet having the right to some privacy. They also talked about not telling people outside the group what members had said. They agreed that if they really had to tell someone else about events in group sessions then they must discuss who they were telling and why with the other group members. This gave the worker the permission she needed to protect the children and their siblings in the event of their making further disclosures during group sessions. It also had the advantage of alerting the worker if at any stage either girl was placed under pressure by their care-givers to give an account of what had happened at the group.

In small groups with only three or four members the absence of a couple of participants will be keenly felt. However in the case of pairing when one child cannot attend a session the leader reverts to giving the other an individual interview. As individual work should already be familiar to these clients this is usually a positive experience. There is, however, considerable difficulty if after a short while one child withdraws. The remaining youngster may feel that he or she has done something wrong, compounding his or her sense of rejection. It is therefore better to plan a limited number of meetings, perhaps two, to begin with. Assuming these are successful the leaders can suggest two further meetings, repeating this process until they sense that the youngsters are so committed to the group that longer-term planning is feasible. Alternatively the leaders may feel that one child is reluctant to attend, in which case they can terminate the group in an ostensibly planned way.

Pairing is useful not only in alleviating the isolation of older children but also in helping younger children who have been physically or emotionally deprived and restricted. Some youngsters may have been so neglected or so inhibited by punitive parents that they have yet to learn to play, explore and experiment. Once they have learnt to play with toys and materials under the guidance of adults, the next big step is to play with other children. Pairing can bridge the gap between the comfortable but limited nature of individual play and the daunting prospect of participating in larger groups.

Family groups

Work can be undertaken with a group of children from the same family where there are three or four children within an age range of about five years. Once these children feel fairly comfortable about their situation they can be matched to a similar set of siblings. This results in a group of between six to eight children. It is difficult to assimilate three or four children from the same family into a group where all the other members are individuals rather than sibling groups. But in this way the two sets of children have a richer experience than they would otherwise have if they were only offered help in their own family group.

One advantage is that there is an almost ready-made group. There is little of the initial awkwardness associated with half a dozen strange children meeting one another for the first time. The time required for the usual preliminaries such as learning each other's names is cut by more than half. Another important advantage is that the youngsters learn that theirs is not the only family with problems of abuse.

One possible drawback is that the two different families will remain separate and the group will not coalesce, however in practice this does not seem to happen. After a brief initial period new alliances are made which cut across the two families. Nevertheless care has to be taken to ensure that the families are compatible and their structure suitable. It would probably not be appropriate to link a family with only one girl with another family with all boys, leaving the one girl without a female ally.

Both 'pairing' and 'family group' work can be used to help with problems other than those of abuse. Children who have suffered a significant bereavement may at some stage be reassured by meeting other youngsters or a family in similar circumstances.

Groups for younger children

There are many principles of group work which apply to all groups whatever the age of the participants. These again are well documented in the standard works mentioned earlier. This section will therefore examine areas specific to group work with young abused children.

Planning and preparation

The main feature of group work with young children is that it will certainly be noisy and possibly messy. Because of this the room for meetings has to be chosen with care. It is likely that such a group will run during the day rather than in the evening. This means that either the room has to be sound-proof or well away from other people who are trying to work – unless you have remarkably tolerant colleagues. The room should be fairly easy to clean, while time has to be allowed for clearing up any mess.

Adult groups may need little more than a suitable room, chairs, a table, pens and paper; with younger clients many more materials will be required. Toys, paints, modelling clay, a mirror and dressing-up clothes are all likely to be used. As with individual work, toys and materials that are not for use in a session should be kept out of sight, otherwise they become an irresistible distraction for the young participants.

The optimum size is probably about six although two adults may cope with as many as eight children. Usually it is necessary to have two adults in charge especially if the children need accompanying to the toilet. One male and one female leader is preferable. Youngsters who have been abused by, say, their mother will learn through the female worker that women can be kind and caring, while if they have been protected to some extent by their father they may be reassured by the presence in the group of a male helper. The two leaders represent a mother and a father figure and this may be the first time that some of the children experience such adults communicating and showing respect for each other without either shouting or physical violence.

In groups with small children the leaders should be directive, ensuring that the sessions do not run out of control and taking the burden of decision making away from the children. Ruth McKnight, a group worker, writes of her early experience of leading children's groups:

> My first lesson was in direct connection with my role. My experiences hitherto had been of discussion groups with a self-effacing sort of leader who was almost one of the group. The children, in fact, taught me that this was impossible in our setting and moreover it was not what they wanted. (McKnight, 1972, p. 136)

Having said this the children should be included in some decision making, for example they may express a preference for refreshments at the beginning of the session rather than halfway through, or they may be consulted about introducing a new member to the group.

The leaders should be able to refer to a group work consultant who will help them evaluate what is happening because young children's groups are fairly boisterous and it is easy for the adults to be distracted from the main issues by particularly demanding or difficult behaviour on the part of one or two youngsters. The consultant needs to be knowledgeable about group dynamics, play work, child abuse and normal child development. The leaders should also be supervised, possibly by the consultant but preferably by a separate supervisor who will negotiate boundaries of responsibility with the consultant.

Other arrangements which have to be sorted out before sessions begin are transport, refreshments, recording, and timing. An additional issue is the decision over whether or not the group is a closed one or whether it will accept new members. Similarly leaders have to decide whether it will be an open-ended group or, if not, how many sessions will be held. On the whole for small children a closed group with a fairly limited number of sessions is most appropriate.

Another important aspect of planning is liaison and confidentiality. Children attending the group should have their own individual worker who will help with practical arrangements and may be providing a child with individual therapy. Depending on the circumstances the worker might be given full details of the child's progress or on the other hand may only be told that the child attended the session. Evidently if during a group session the child discloses something which indicates that he or any other person is in danger then the leaders *must* ensure that a protective agency is informed.

In selecting group members there are few hard and fast rules although it is necessary to avoid including either a very disturbed, disruptive child or a child who is obviously very different from the other members such as one girl in a group of seven boys. Ruth McKnight makes the point that:

> One thing we have found as the result of hard experience is that it is unwise to include an extremely disturbed child in the group. The inclusion of such a child too early, and too quickly, leads to him becoming the immediate scapegoat, which can be harmful for the child and the group. It takes a very great deal of skilled manoeuvring to retrieve this situation. We tend to work with such a child by means of face-to-face play situations instead. When the child has worked through some of his problems we may transfer him to a group situation later. (McKnight, 1972, p. 134)

Despite this, children who are used to coping in other groups as the only one with certain characteristics can be included. One example is that of a handicapped child who attends a mainstream school.

Mixing boys with girls is perfectly feasible but there will be some difficulties particularly with the seven plus ages when boys begin to have a poor opinion of girls and vice versa. It helps in this age group if the girls are a little older than the boys. Workers unused to group work with children would do well to start with single sex groups and only tackle mixed groups once their skills and confidence increase.

One feature of small children's groups is that there is likely to be an informal group of parents, caregivers and social workers waiting in a nearby room. This occurs because the children are too young to bring themselves to sessions and because they have a right to have a reassuring familiar adult to hand in the event of their becoming distressed. If the needs of this informal group of carers are overlooked they may well sabotage the efforts of the leaders by becoming noisy or demanding their attention before and after sessions. Eileen Vizard and colleagues solved this problem by evolving:

> the practice of having the little children's group and the caretakers group amalgamate for part of the last session, in order to sit down together and watch extracts from the video of the children during the preceeding five weeks. This has turned out to be a great success and very popular. (Vizard, 1987, p. 18)

Finally there is nothing more daunting or confusing for a small child than to find that having been prepared for a group experience he or she is sitting alone with a couple of equally bewildered group leaders. It is important to ensure that attendances are confirmed and that at least three or four children arrive together to attend the first session.

The first session

With young children the first group session is of crucial importance. Older clients, who dislike the first meeting, may be persuaded to return in the hopes of matters improving. Small children who do not enjoy themselves on the first occasion often resist any attempts to involve them in subsequent meetings.

Adults meeting for the first time in a group usually start by becoming acquainted with each other's names. In the case of young children it is more important to familiarise them with the physical surroundings first. They will need to know the whereabouts of the toilet and how to reach their mother/familiar adult if they become distressed. They will also want to play with any toys present.

Once members have satisfied their curiosity about their surroundings they can be properly introduced to the grown-ups and other children in the group. Sometimes name labels are used. Various games can help children learn each other's names. One example is to have several funny hats which children put on each other's heads. The recipient of the hat says, 'Thank you, I'm Sue' (or whatever their name is). Once the members know each other's names they can practise by saying, 'Here you are, Sue' when they put a hat on someone's head. Another idea is a game of catch, where a participant throws a ball of socks or bean bag to another child whose name the thrower remembers and calls out. The leaders will join in these games to ensure that no child is embarrassed due to possessing 'butter fingers', a poor memory or a forgettable name.

The next important part of the first session is the drawing up of a set of group rules and some sharing of why the children are attending.

The members need to know what they can expect of the group and what the group expects of them. The children should help in the task of formulating the rules and, as illustrated by the list given by the pair group, they will enjoy the inclusion of a few 'adult' rules such as 'no smoking'.

Suggested activities

The activities of the group will depend largely on its objectives. A group for neglected, understimulated children may start by encouraging children to explore different play materials such as sand, water, clay and finger paints. It will then move on to activities which require a joint effort such as a group collage or building a structure together. For these children having a meal together, sitting at a table using cutlery and saying, 'Please' and 'Thank you' may be important learning experiences.

A group for those who have been subjected to physical violence will focus on helping them recognise that they should not feel guilty and ashamed. They can be invited to dress up and act out famous stories of children who have been mistreated such as Cinderella, Oliver Twist and Jane Eyre. Through role-play they can be encouraged to avoid provocative or 'victim' behaviour. The members may also need to act out angry, violent emotions, through destructive games, mock fights and throwing cushions or bean bags at hated objects. Eventually through co-operative, construction games, a group collage perhaps, they can be shown how much more can be achieved by peaceful means.

Groups for sexually abused children will need to provide outlets for angry feelings. Furthermore their members may be very bewildered about what has happened to them. For such children, unlike physically abused and neglected youngsters, there are few fairy-tales or stories about sexually abused children with whom they can identify. They may need some simple sex education in order to make sense of their experiences. But first they will need to share a vocabulary in order to communicate their experiences. In an early session the members can be encouraged to shout out their own name for the private parts of their body. They learn by this means that everybody uses 'rude' words. The exercise also gives them access to a wide range of terms to describe what has happened to them.

The participants in such a group can be encouraged to value their body and assert their right not to be molested. This can be done through role-play and by using a mirror, in front of which the children stand and declare, 'It's my body' and 'No, go away'. The more confident children can accompany the diffident ones and help them say the words.

Abused children, whatever the nature of the mistreatment, share many negative feelings. They all have to learn to develop trust and there are games which help in this endeavour. In one game members close their eyes and allow themselves to fall backwards in order to be caught by other group members. In the case of small children who have limitations of strength and co-ordination it will be advisable for the adults to take the role of catcher; dropping your partner defeats the object of the exercise!

Activities suggested in the section on individual work can be adapted to group sessions. One example, already described, involves sketching expressions on blank faces, the children are then asked to share their drawings and say what makes them feel sad, happy, angry, ashamed or afraid. Finally, it should be noted that young children do not appreciate abstract concepts so all ideas have to be illustrated in concrete form by the use of dolls, puppets, drawings, stories and games.

Groups for older children and teenagers

Much of the previous section on groups for younger children will also apply to those for older ones. For example, the optimum size will still be six plus leaders (although there have been a number of successful groups with only three or four youngsters). This section will therefore simply highlight some of the important features of group work with older abused children.

Planning and preparation

Older children who have been abused for sometime will have had longer than little children to develop a mistrust of adults, longer to adapt to the victim role and longer to harbour feelings of anger, worthlessness and fear. There is likely to be considerable testing of the trustworthiness of the leaders and of the group boundaries. It is essential to have two leaders, one of whom should be experienced in group work and both of whom must be emotionally resilient. It is also essential that both workers are supervised and well supported, with both supervisor and group consultant available to give assistance.

It is again helpful to have a therapist of each sex, to present a model of adult men and women working harmoniously together and to provide an outlet for the youngsters' feelings about women/mothers and men/fathers. When helping sexually-abused girls the male worker is likely to be subjected to periods of severe testing and provocative behaviour. In one group comprised of four teenage girls the male leader had to cope with cushions thrown at him, questions about his sexual prowess and 'accusations' of homosexuality when he did not respond to their sexual invitations. In another group 'The girls were often very angry with the male therapist and expressed suspicion about his motives in running the group' (Furniss *et al.*, 1988, p. 102).

Teenagers can be shy and self-conscious. It will be difficult for them to pluck up the courage to attend the initial meeting by themselves. It may be helpful for them to come to a couple of preliminary meetings accompanied by their social worker who will stay for the first few informal gatherings. Alternatively, members can meet each other in pairs on a casual basis prior to the initial group session so that when they do arrive for the first meeting they feel they are coming with a 'friend'.

The first session

Older children, in contrast to younger ones, are likely to show more interest in their fellow group members than in their physical surroundings although soon after their arrival they will need to know where they can put their coats and go to the toilet. But they will be curious about the other participants' names and experiences.

One useful exercise involves finding out the meanings of members' given names. This helps them to learn both each other's names and also something about themselves. It is fun and flattering for a David to learn that his name means 'beloved', for a Claire to hear she is 'bright' or a Tammy find out that she is 'perfection'. Youngsters who have an unusual or less popular name may well be encouraged to learn that it has a pleasant meaning such as Beatrice being 'bringer of joy' or Cyril 'lordly'. The leaders will however need to ensure that they do not cause distress to those whose names have less desirable connotations such as Doreen 'sullen', Elvis 'old noise' or Cameron 'crooked nose'.

Suggested activities

Again activities will depend on the objectives of the group. A group for physically abused, violent, teenage boys may concentrate on the youngsters playing snooker without coming to blows or learning to trust adults, their companions and their own abilities through an activity such as rock climbing or sailing.

Unless the objective of the group is purely social or narrowly task-focused on an issue unrelated to abuse, the youngsters should be helped to find a way to share their experiences. They can be invited to choose how to talk about the abuse to which they were subjected.

They may decide to face the wall or window or try to give an account following the rules of a game like 'Just A Minute' – without repetition, hesitation or deviation.

Activities with paints, pens and paper prove useful and popular. A group collage or painting helps participants to express their feelings about themselves and the group without being alone in the spotlight. It also assists in the process of group cohesion. Discussion can be encouraged through paintings and drawings which are described to other group members.

Filling in a questionnaire is another activity which can help spark-off discussions and it seems to hold an attraction for adolescents. The objective of much group work is a change of attitudes, especially self-denigrating ones. The use of a questionnaire at one of the earliest sessions and again at the last provides a means of evaluating the effectiveness of the group and gives members an insight into their own progress.

Some of the activities, such as role-play, suggested in the section on individual work and on groups for younger children can prove useful in groups for older ones. This includes play and games. So many abused teenagers will have lost the opportunity to play in a happy, carefree environment. Some of the joy of being an irresponsible child can be recaptured by holding the meetings in rooms with toys available or arranging parties and outings to perhaps fairs or children's films. The members should, however, have a choice in such activities because adolescents may well resent being treated in a juvenile fashion when they are aspiring towards adulthood.

Finally, the use of video equipment has proved very successful with these groups. Young people are, despite some shyness, eager for feedback on the way they look and behave. Re-playing a video film of part of a session provides uncritical, objective feedback. The members may at first express some reluctance to be filmed in which case persuasion can be tried, but a video should not be used without the group's ultimate agreement.

6

Substitute Care

When children die at the hands of their parents the inevitable questions are raised such as 'Why wasn't he taken out of the home?' or 'Why was she allowed to go home?' The solution to child abuse seems so simple – children must be rescued from abusive parents and placed with carers who will not harm them. Unfortunately the answer is not so easy. This chapter examines some of the problems, complexities and benefits of removing abused children from their homes. It does not however aim to cover all aspects of substitute care; there are already comprehensive works on the topic (e.g. DHSS, 1976; Thoburn, 1988).

The problems of substitute care

One of the main problems associated with substitute care is that of finding the right placement for the child in question. This is a problem encountered with all youngsters, not just abused ones, in need of a foster home. Too often they have to move from one short-term placement to another. This problem is described in an account by Phil Quinn of Peter, a boy who initially came into care because his mother, on her own with three children, became ill:

> So began the progression of foster homes for Peter, usually at two- or three-month intervals. He lived in several different foster homes during the two-year period following the break-up of his family. . . . Each move became more painful than the last because each convinced the boy that no one loved him or wanted him. (Quinn, 1988, p. 47)

Although abused children share this problem of changing placements, they have additional difficulties arising from, and associated with the fact they have been mistreated.

Legacy of the Stockholm syndrome

The Stockholm syndrome and its relevance to abused children was discussed in Chapter 1. The loyalty and attachment exhibited by some hostages towards their captors is reflected in a similar loyalty and attachment shown by mistreated children towards their abusers. A seven-year-old, Eva, had been rejected at birth by her mother. Subsequently she had been physically and emotionally abused to the extent that she was stunted in growth and had evidence of injuries. Eva expressed adoration of her mother and resisted removal into care. Her first two sets of substitute carers rejected her. Then she went to live with Mr and Mrs K who were loving, experienced foster parents. Nevertheless, after a weekend visit home she refused to pack her case when she had to return to Mr and Mrs K.

After an unsuccessful return home-on-trial, Mr and Mrs K campaigned for her to be returned to them. They succeeded and eventually Eva, having acknowledged that she could not go back to her parents, settled happily with Mr and Mrs K. This couple was able to understand the little girl's attachment to her home and gave her unconditional love. Unfortunately not all foster parents have the emotional resilience of Mr and Mrs K. Faced with a child who seems to lavish all her love on 'undeserving' abusive parents, foster parents may become frustrated as the child continues to reject their kindness and care; this in fact happened in Eva's first two placements.

Reactions of abused children to care

Many abused children do not want to leave their home, they simply want the abuse to stop and to be loved by their parents. Sarah, it will be recalled, did not see boarding school as an escape. Instead she looked forward to each holiday, hoping that 'this time it will be all right'. Again, Chapter 1 demonstrated that the need of children to belong to their family is strong. They live, ever-hopeful of 'deserving' their parents' love.

Littner found that foster children often believe they have been rejected by their parents because they were bad (Littner, 1956). Emily McFadden describes the experience of one set of foster parents:

> Mr and Mrs Pike said that they carefully observed 4-year-old Sam playing in a corner with his Teddy bear. Whispering Sam told his Teddy bear 'If you wet the bed the police will take you away'. Sam slapped the bear, then threw it.
> 'Bad bear now you have to go away'. (McFadden, 1980)

Many social workers have been greeted with 'If you don't behave the social worker will take you away'. Elizabeth Timberlake demonstrated that the feeling of guilt and responsibility for removal from home is greater in abused children. These youngsters were more likely to connect the reason for their placement in care with their own behaviour while non-abused children associated it with a crisis event (Timberlake, 1979). The involvement of the police and the use of formal legal processes and the courts, although probably necessary, all serve to enhance an abused child's sense of wrongdoing.

Even as an adult Sarah is adamant that she would not have wished to be taken into care. The task of fitting into a new family with its different mores and ways of interacting would have been too difficult for her. Furthermore when young she assumed that all fathers beat their children and would have expected any foster parents to do so. Both Marie and Sarah recalled being able to anticipate their father's behaviour and 'keep one step ahead of him'. They felt safer with the 'devil' they knew. Not only will such youngsters feel very fearful of an unknown new situation they will also expect mistreatment and rejection. If they cannot win the love of those parents who should, because of the blood-tie or legal adoption, love them, what hope have they of winning the love of any other carers?

When taken into care each abused child will have his or her own way of adapting to family or residential situations. Some may behave as well as possible, still hoping that by being good they may win a little of their carers' love. Phil Quinn describes what happened to Peter when he was eventually placed with adoptive parents who started to beat him:

> Peter became hyper-alert to the wants and desires of his adoptive parents. He knew what had happened that day could happen again. He did not blame his [adoptive] mother for losing her temper with him. After all, it only confirmed what he already believed about himself – he was bad and deserved punishment. He tried to atone for his evilness by catering to their every wish, bringing them coffee in bed, preparing dinner, running errands, doing anything to try to get them to like him and not to hurt him again (Quinn, 1988, p. 126).

Other children will be very withdrawn and will retreat to their rooms whenever tension builds within the home. Foster parents have also reported difficulties coping with children whose behaviour is provocative. Emily McFadden reporting on a training course for foster parents, when describing patterns of adaptive behaviour, wrote:

> One obvious pattern is that of the "provoker" who seems to be asking for punishment. To illustrate this pattern the instructor often uses the

example of 6-year-old Melinda who kicks the foster mother and says "Go ahead and hit me". Class members then discuss the motivations for such behaviour and why it is important to help Melinda change her behaviour. Often, foster parents will say that they now realize that they have allowed themselves to be provoked by such behaviour – and have, in fact maintained the pattern by responding with punishment when the child asks for it". (McFadden, 1980)

The reasons for such apparently provocative behaviour are varied. Children cannot believe that the substitute carers will not eventually mistreat them and so they test the limits of the carers' patience and tolerance. Some children find violence, rejection or molestation so familiar that it becomes more reassuring than the unfamiliar kindness and protection. Some youngsters feel they are so wicked that they must be punished and therefore seek punishment. Others were so used to the role of family scapegoat or seducer that they do not know any other role. Sexually abused children might have received love only in return for sexual favours consequently they believe that their foster parents or the residential staff will only care for them if given similar favours.

Children in care may continue to worry about the rest of the family. Marie stated that she would have resisted being taken into care because she would have been too concerned about what would have happened to her mother and siblings. Jessica Cameronchild wrote that, among other factors, being an abused child means 'Hoping maybe you were adopted and that you could find your real parents and convince them you'll be good if only they'll take you back. But worrying about who would take care of your "present" parents if you were rescued' (Cameronchild, 1978).

It is only occasionally that more than two siblings can be placed together in the same foster home, yet attachments to brothers and sisters can be stronger than those to parents. Phil Quinn again describes Peter's feelings when he realised he and his brothers were to be placed in separate foster homes:

As time went by, Peter became more and more interested in his brothers, spending time each day with them. . . . They became the most important people in his life. Then came the day the welfare workers arrived to take the boys to the [separate] foster homes arranged for them. Without hesitation or resistance Peter had gone with Mr White, not knowing that he was being separated from his brothers. . . . It was not until the car began pulling away from the curb that Peter realised what was happening. Like an animal caged for the first time, he was suddenly on all fours searching out his brothers through the rear window of the car. Clawing desperately, he tore at the door trying to get out. (Quinn, 1988, p. 45)

Substitute care-givers

Foster parents and staff in residential homes have to meet many demands made by the youngsters in their care. But in the case of abused children there are additional difficulties. Fears of violence and feelings of rejection are such that any form of punishment may provoke an extreme response. Tom O'Neill describes his brother's feelings when very caring foster parents 'had reason to chide him. They ticked him off and sent him to bed. He went to bed and cried and cried. He cried because they didn't want him. Admittedly, it was only a temporary banishment but to him it was a real rejection' (O'Neill, 1981, p. 75). It is acknowledged that limits have to be set and bad behaviour checked but corporal punishment should be avoided. The bodies of abused children have been sufficiently degraded in the past; in care they have the opportunity to learn that their bodies are worthy of respect. This may cause difficulties in a foster home if the parents are in the habit of hitting their own offspring. An additional concern expressed by foster parents relates to caring for the victims of sexual abuse. Foster fathers in particular may be unsure about how far they can use touch and cuddling to express affection.

Finally, although the majority of foster and residential homes provide an excellent environment, there are cases where a child is abused while in care. Dennis O'Neill was beaten to death by his foster father. His brother, Tom, describes his end:

> He had septic ulcers in his feet. His legs were severely chapped, a condition for which he had received little or no medical attention. His chest was extensively bruised and discoloured. He had recently been beaten on the back with a stick. His stomach contained no trace of food. He was dead. (O'Neill, 1981, p. 68)

Shirley Woodcock (1984) died aged three while in the care of foster parents. The Inquiry Report into her death recorded 'extensive bruising (some 50 bruises in total) which was thought to have been sustained over a period of about 10 days. . . . The post mortem examination indicated they were the result of pinching, prodding gripping and falls' (Woodcock, 1984, p. 19). In 1987 a two-year-old boy in England, originally taken into care as a possible victim of sexual abuse, was killed by his foster father. Incidents of sexual abuse at the hands of foster parents and residential staff emerge at regular intervals. For example, a seven-year-old girl was forced to watch films of child pornography by both her foster father and mother who then made her indulge in the activities shown on the films.

The benefits of substitute care

Despite the problems of substitute care, it can provide children with significant benefits. Residential and foster homes will be required for some time to come.

A safe place

Although a few children sustain serious injuries or die at the hands of substitute carers many more would be killed by their own parents were they not removed from the home. Maria Colwell (1974) and Jasmine Beckford (1985), both subjects of public inquiries, were killed after being returned home despite the misgivings of their foster parents.

Death or severe injury can be caused by starvation or direct blows but death can also arise because it is the only way a child knows how to escape his or her miserable existence. Jessica Cameronchild describes how her younger brother, subjected to severe beatings, having his head shaved and being forced to sleep outside, committed suicide.

> Finally, my brother was again sent home from school, and this time when he arrived home he shot his head off with a rifle. He was eleven years old. There was no question about his death being suicide; he left a note and the trigger was rigged. (Cameronchild, 1978, p. 143)

Marie's eldest sister, we recall, took overdoses of tablets.

Some children die because their attempts to escape abuse lead them into danger. The body of eight-year-old Lester Chapman (1979) was found on 26 February 1978 'Trapped in a sewage sludge at a site 50 yards from the river, about a quarter of a mile from his home. He had died of exposure, almost certainly on the bitter night on which he ran away' (Chapman, 1979, p. 1). Lester had been physically and emotionally abused and had run away from home on three previous occasions. Removal to a loving substitute home may, in similar cases, save lives.

Therapeutic aspects of substitute care

Despite the dangers of emotional abuse due to the vagaries of the care system, children frequently thrive when placed with substitute carers. Tom O'Neill describes the experiences of another of his brothers who, having shared the nightmare of abusing foster parents with Dennis, was then found another home.

From the outset Terry's new foster-family made every effort to give him a
real home – not only material benefits but also the one thing that had been
missing for many years: love. He was accepted as part of the family. It
turned out to be one of the happiest periods in the whole of his lifetime.
(O'Neill, 1981, p. 74)

One important benefit given by substitute carers is that they can
provide an alternative model of family life. Many foster homes show
abused children that instead of violence and recrimination between
husband and wife there is companionship and respect. The youngsters learn to feel safe and protected by adults. They acquire self-
control and discipline through praise, encouragement and gentle
correction. They begin to realise that the love of parent for child is
unconditional. All this will help them to become better partners and
parents themselves if they choose, in later life, to have their own
family.

One of the best therapies for abused children is to be in an
environment where they can express feelings without fearing the
consequences, where they are helped to feel valued, attractive and
capable. A very low self-esteem is one of the main results of being
abused. Foster parents and residential staff can do much to make
good the damage to a youngster's view of him or herself.

Early removal

There are a number of cases usually in the form of neglect or repeated
physical injury to very young babies which require the early and
permanent removal of infants. Sometimes parents find themselves
unable to love one particular child. The reasons for this bonding
failure are many and varied; sometimes the cause remains a mystery.
A difficult birth, one coinciding with a family crisis, neonatal
separation and a baby of the 'wrong' sex are all thought to be
contributory factors. Some parents, given support and counselling
can grow to love the baby but others fail to do so. In the latter case the
child should be removed from the home as soon as possible.

There are other parents so limited in ability and so emotionally
handicapped that they are unable to give any child unconditional
affection. They consistently put their own needs before those of their
offspring and despite considerable assistance show no change in
attitude or functioning. Again the child should be removed as soon as
possible – at birth if necessary, because it is continuing abuse that
imprisons children in a dependent but damaging relationship with
their parents. A small baby is more readily adopted than an older
child who already has the physical or emotional scars of abuse.

It is recognised that early removal is no easy decision. Many social workers will have had experience of families in which the prospects for a new baby were very bleak, yet given help the parents have tapped dormant personal resources to provide an environment in which their offspring have been able to thrive. Professionals involved with abuse cases need to develop assessment skills and then, for the sake of the children, act on that assessment.

Overcoming the problems

It would seem at first sight that the disadvantages of substitute care outweigh the advantages. Yet the balance can be made a little more even through various strategies which can help overcome potential problems.

Preparation

Foster parents and residential staff, required to look after mistreated children, can as already noted encounter a wide range of difficulties from anger felt towards the abusive parents to finding that they too are prompted to abuse the child. Because of this foster parents and residential staff should be carefully selected and trained for work with abused children. Emily McFadden describes a course on 'Fostering the Battered and Abused Child' designed for experienced foster parents who have already received training on child development and the impact of separation. It is a twenty-hour, eight-week course combining formal instruction with informal discussion and experiential learning techniques (McFadden, 1980). This is by no means the only such course but many authorities still only provide general training or a one-off session on abuse to both foster parents and residential staff then wonder why there are so many unsuccessful placements.

Children coming into care should also be as well prepared as possible. Ideally, before being placed they should be helped to understand why they are being removed from home and to appreciate that it is not their fault. They have done nothing to deserve the mistreatment and rejection by their parents. Furthermore when they move from one substitute home to another they need to be told why. Tom O'Neill describes the experience of three of his brothers:

> They had to leave this foster-home. They didn't know why. They had done nothing wrong. Why did no one tell them why they had to go? They were happy there. Could no one have soothed the hurt they were experiencing by just telling them why it had to be as it was? (O'Neill, 1981, p. 61)

Children fear the unknown. Tom O'Neill again describes how Terry cried out, 'Don't let them take me away, Dad' as he was carried from the house where he had suffered savage mistreatment and witnessed the killing of his brother, Dennis. 'He cried out because of the dire consequences that had been instilled into him of being removed' (O'Neill, 1981, p. 66). Children can be helped to overcome this fear by being gradually introduced to their new family if circumstances allow. When children have to be removed in haste then they can at least be shown photographs of their new home and be provided with a verbal description. If time is short this can be given in the car on the way to the house. Every social worker responsible for the removal of children should have 24-hour access to a set of photographs and a video or audio tape recording of the activities and people in each foster and residential home that an authority is likely to use.

Wherever possible the natural parents (this phrase includes adoptive or step-parents to whom the child is attached) should also be prepared for the child's removal. They should be partners with the professional workers and substitute care-givers in planning for the future of their offspring. Parental participation in the decision-making process is important and includes attending at least part of any case conference in which recommendations for removal are made. If parents are made to feel angry by the actions of protective agencies they are likely to turn some of that anger against the child. Consequently they may refuse to visit him or to give help by, for example, providing photographs for a life-story book.

Maintaining contact

There are considerable benefits in maintaining contact between abused children and their families. The youngsters will worry less about their parents and siblings if they can see them at regular intervals. Thoburn notes: 'All studies which have specifically assessed the well-being of children in long-term foster care have concluded that in the majority of cases well-being is enhanced if the children have regular contact with their birth families' (Thoburn, 1988, p. 48).

Many families although physically separated can be kept together in spirit by frequent letters, phone calls and access visits. Grandparents, other relatives and family friends can also make a youngster feel valued and less rejected by being encouraged to keep in touch, remember birthdays and perhaps send presents on special occasions.

The parents and others may need help to maintain contact. Wendy, a twelve-year-old, was ill-treated by her mother, and her father felt he could not cope with the situation. She came into care and was placed in a small children's home. At first her father refused to visit. The social worker was sure that he had a lot of affection for his daughter. She spent time with him discussing the importance of family contact. It slowly emerged that the father felt so ashamed of failing to cope with the situation that he was too embarrassed to visit the home. The social worker, understanding this, arranged for access visits on neutral ground. She continued to help the father appreciate that he had done his best in a difficult situation. Eventually, with self-esteem restored, he visited the home and access visits became frequent. The social worker also showed acceptance of the mother's difficulties. Wendy was delighted the following Christmas when she received a card from her mother inside which were the words 'love from mum'.

Access visits can sometimes be unsatisfactory with all parties feeling that the situation is artificial but at least the children remain in contact with the important people in their lives. Now and then children become distressed by the visits and an assessment has to be made as to whether this is due to the youngster's aversion to access or distress at not being at home with the parents. Occasionally children are re-abused during access visits. A father who had raped his daughter was allowed supervised access. Their social worker regularly took them swimming. The girl eventually plucked up the courage to tell her foster mother that her natural father had come into her changing cubicle at the baths and had molested her again. If, because of the risk of re-abuse or for some other reason, access is not possible then phone calls, letters, exchange of video or audio-tapes and photographs are all ways in which families can keep in touch.

Another now well-accepted method of helping youngsters to keep in touch with their family and their origins is through a life-story book. This involves recording important events in the child's history illustrated by documents and photographs. Experience has shown that a loose-leaf book is preferable because additional information about the youngster's early life can be inserted at a later date. As far as possible this is a task undertaken as a partnership between the child and his or her key worker. The child should be given the choice of whether the accounts of events are written in the first or third person, for example, 'My first school' or 'Sean's first school'.

Although the placement of siblings in separate foster homes was identified as a problem this is not always the case. If siblings can remain in touch through the means already suggested they can sometimes benefit from being given individual care. Lucille was the eldest in her family. Her mother became very ill and Lucille, at the tender age of seven, took over the care of her four younger brothers. Her father began to abuse the children. After disclosure she was placed in a foster home with some of her brothers. She failed to settle.

She was then found a home with foster parents who only had older daughters. There Lucille learnt to be a dependent child and was delighted to be relieved of the burden of responsibility for her brothers. Nevertheless arrangements were made for her to see her parents and siblings as often as possible.

Continued assistance

It is tempting for hard-pressed social workers to remove a child from a dangerous household, breathe a sigh of relief and turn attention to those cases where children remain in an 'at risk' situation at home. But this simple rescue is inadequate. However good the new substitute parents are the youngster will need help in overcoming the negative effects of mistreatment.

Foster parents may find it easy to welcome or at least tolerate the continuing involvement of natural parents when removal from home becomes necessary due to illness, overwhelming problems or difficult behaviour in the child. It is not so easy to accept a parent who has injured an attractive, appealing toddler or raped a shy, affectionate six-year-old. Foster and natural parents may have conflicting attitudes to child rearing and there may be unjustifiable criticism arising from class or cultural differences. This is illustrated by the case of Jasmine Beckford (1985) and her sister, Louise. The foster parents complained about the state in which the girls returned to them after access visits to the parental home. 'There were also frequent complaints about the clothes often being dirty and smelly, and about the greasing of the children's hair. It is normal practice to grease and plait Afro-hair. The social worker felt that the girls were, in fact, returned clean and that their hair had an acceptable amount of grease for the culture involved' (Beckford, 1985, p. 109).

Residential staff, foster and natural parents all need continued counselling to accept or at least understand each others' values and perspectives. There is nothing worse for the children than to be surrounded by adults in conflict. Their loyalty will be divided and they will no doubt feel responsible for the situation. It is particularly important that the foster parents and residential staff say nothing derogatory about the children's family, which, as indicated in Chapter 1, forms part of the youngster's identity.

It is imperative to keep all parties informed of plans for the children's futures. Uncertainty will lead to anxiety and resentment. In the case of Jasmine Beckford the foster parents believed that the two girls were to remain with them permanently. They accused the social workers of leaving them out of any rehabilitation schemes and taking the two sisters away 'abruptly'. Their complaints although not strictly accurate reflect the way that poor communications between social workers and themselves led to the feeling that neither they nor the needs of the children had been properly considered.

Returning home

Sometimes children thought to have been abused are removed from home by emergency procedures or through parental request. They then have to be returned home because, despite professional misgivings, there is insufficient evidence of abuse to convince a court that the child is in need of further protection. Cases of sexual abuse, where there is no medical evidence plus a total denial by the alleged perpetrator, are very nearly impossible to prove. Physical injury especially on older youngsters is often viewed by courts as acceptable chastisement. Emotional abuse and neglect can rarely be demonstrated until the child's plight becomes extreme. A return home from care should be carefully planned but, usually for legal reasons, this is not always possible.

When children remain at home or return to it after a period in care, the authorities have varying degrees of control. In order to achieve legal sanction and control in difficult cases the initial investigative and assessment state is of crucial importance. There are a number of works which contain sections on investigation and assessment (e.g. Jones *et al.*, 1987 and Cooper and Ball, 1987). There is no need here to cover the ground which they have already examined. However, one or two comments about techniques and factors involved in the assessment process should be made. They may prove useful in the examination of the situation before removing a child as well as in the evaluation of plans for rehabilitation.

Assessment techniques

The growth chart – children who have been abused sometimes fail to put on sufficient weight and height despite the fact that their families are of average build and there is no growth impairing disease or physical condition present. A child's physical progress can be monitored through the use of growth charts. Height, weight and head circumference can be recorded on these. They are best used by medical staff, who can interpret them correctly and who have access to the same scales and measuring devices every time. They should sign the chart by each measurement, in case they are asked in court to confirm it. But it is the responsibility of the social worker to request that such charts are kept when a problem is suspected. Growth charts are now much more familiar to non-medical personnel because mothers of newborn infants are often given booklets in which to record their babies' progress and these contain simple charts.

Children who have failed to thrive due to abuse frequently put on weight once placed in a caring residential or foster home. If the child is returned home charts should be used to ensure that growth continues at a satisfactory rate. Jasmine Beckford was returned from care only to be killed by her step-father. She was four years old at the time of her death. The inquiry report records that when she was discharged from hospital after being taken into care she weighed 18 lb 5 oz. Seven months later, when she was reunited with her parents after being fostered she weighed 25 lb 5 oz. She died, 27 months later, weighing 23 lb. The inquiry report states: 'The failure of Area 6 to take particular note of Jasmine's weight over the three years of a Care Order is perhaps the most striking, single aspect of child abuse that was fatally neglected' (Beckford, 1985, p. 114).

Flow charts – these are lists and dates of all the injuries or abusive incidents to a child. In a separate column other important events are recorded in a way that matches dates, incidents and events. It is a simple exercise but can be remarkably effective in demonstrating patterns of abuse. Practitioners on seeing these charts have made comments such as: 'The incidents seem to occur at regular intervals' or 'I didn't realise she had had so many hospital admissions in only sixteen weeks'.

Written contracts – these are often used when parental care is below an acceptable standard. Parents are sometimes confused about professional expectations and may not for example take a child to nursery because they do not appreciate the importance of this in the eyes of the professionals involved. A written contract of both the behaviour expected of the parent and the commitment the family can expect from the professional agencies ensures that children are not unnecessarily removed from home or prevented from returning to their family due to confusion and mis-communication. It is, however, important that the parents understand the words used. Care has to be taken not to cause additional problems for parents with reading difficulties, while those whose first language is different from that of the practitioners should be provided with a good translation. Older youngsters, beginning to take responsibility for their own behaviour may also be involved in forming a contract with the parents and workers.

The views of children

In any plans for rehabilitation account must be taken of the views of the children. However, extreme caution has to be exercised in the interpretation of children's verbal and non-verbal communications. Terry O'Neill's 'Don't let them take me away, dad' could so easily have been interpreted as a real desire to stay with the foster father who had killed his brother, Dennis. Sarah's crying was seen as evidence of her homesickness by the boarding-school staff.

Some children have no idea what is in their interests but many, like Wendy, the twelve-year-old we have already met, know exactly what is best for them. Nevertheless workers can unwittingly influence their clients as June Thorburn warns:

> Often you will become a very important person to the youngster, who will very much want to please you. Since your job is to help prepare a plan which you believe has most chance of meeting the child's needs, there is some risk that your enthusiasm for the plan will communicate itself in such a way that he or she will be reluctant to express any doubts . . . several youngsters whose workers were convinced that they wished to be adopted, conveyed to our research psychologist that they had severe doubts. (Thoburn, 1988, p. 33)

Other indications

Other factors which will indicate that rehabilitation may be a viable alternative include a positive change in parental attitudes towards the child, an acceptance that they, not the child, are responsible for the abuse and an ability to relate to professional helpers as partners in planning for their youngster's future. If problems such as overcrowding, alcohol abuse or marital violence were factors which triggered the abuse then improvement in these areas will be required before rehabilitation can be considered.

Social workers are responsible for preparing everyone for the return home. This includes the siblings who have remained at home throughout. They may resent the intrusion of the abused child and the adjustments such as losing a bedroom to themselves when rehabilitation takes place. The substitute caregivers and other professionals should also be able to appreciate the reasons for the return home decision. The child may create problems for the parents simply because both child and family may have difficulties making the necessary adjustments and because the child is anxious and insecure. The parents need to be prepared for these eventualities while the youngster ought to be made fully aware of what is happening and should be re-introduced at a pace which suits him or her.

Finally, an ability to maintain changes and improvements and to cope with the adjustments required should be monitored once the

child is back with parents. This can be through supervision and a
'home-on-trial' period. But in any such arrangement it is imperative
that the workers involved communicate regularly with the child as
well as with the parents; simply *seeing* the child is not enough.

7

Preventing Child Abuse

The longer-term effects of child abuse will be discussed in the next chapter. Whatever the implications of abuse for the victim's future, no child should have to experience the pain and degradation experienced by Marie, Helen and Sarah. Moreover the more longstanding the abuse the more children are likely to be imprisoned by their situation. They may have become attached to the perpetrator, resist removal into care and be trapped in a maelstrom of negative feelings. Because of this the phrase 'prevention is better than cure' is nowhere more applicable than it is in relation to the abuse of children.

This chapter will discuss prevention in terms of a number of projects designed to help prevent child abuse and also in terms of socioeconomic factors. Some of the measures outlined are directed towards parents despite the focus of this book being on the child. This is because, especially in the case of babies and young children, there is very little that youngsters can do to protect themselves; it is the responsibility of the parents to keep them safe.

There are very many projects designed to prevent abuse. Some are aimed at families in general, others involve identifying 'at risk' situations. Provision may be through state authorities such as local social services departments or through charitable, private or voluntary enterprises. It is not possible to include all the projects in this chapter; a number have been selected for comment.

Parenthood in perspective

Neglect and abuse often arise not because the parents are deliberately cruel or uncaring but simply because they lack the knowledge that would enable them to understand the needs of their offspring and respond appropriately to them. The phrase 'unrealistic expectations' is frequently used to describe abusing parents' attitude to their children. However, the unrealism of their expectations is often due to ignorance rather than malice. For example, a mother who becomes angry when trying, unsuccessfully, to toilet train her nine-month-old infant needs to learn that babies aged under eighteen months rarely have the muscular control required to use a potty properly.

A high proportion of school-children are likely to start their own families within about ten years of leaving school. Even those who do not have offspring may well have some involvement with children through perhaps babysitting for friends. There is therefore an advantage to be gained by starting some form of preparation for parenthood in schools. This should not consist simply of 'how to bath a baby' and other physical aspects of care, important though these are. Youngsters need to be helped to look at the hard work and sacrifices required of parents, not to mention the financial implications of starting a family. Advertisements for baby products show laughing, cherubic infants, however even the most delightful of babies can rapidly become a wet, cross, smelly, screaming bundle. An essential part of the school curriculum should be Human Development. This will help future parents to appreciate that a toddler's apparent disobedience is really an attempt to sort out boundaries and the truculence of an adolescent is the natural result of growing independence.

One example of an attempt to bring reality to the parents of the future is a video called 'Parenthood in Perspective'. It is designed for showing in British schools. It demonstrates the problems as well as the joys of parenthood. There are now a number of similar 'preparation for parenthood' schemes in schools. Unfortunately some of these are aimed predominantly at the less academic female pupils and yet abusers may be educated, professional people. An example is that of the family of Max Piazzani (1974) a small boy killed by his parents. The report of the Inquiry into his death notes 'The father in this case is an educated Italian and the mother is a music teacher who had regular pupils coming to the house' (Piazzani, 1974, p. 8). Moreover, as many boys as girls will grow up to abuse children. Therefore all young people should be included in parenthood classes.

One of the problems of any learning in school is that unless it is carried on outside and after school it may be forgotten. In America many organisations are formally engaged in educating parents about child rearing (Brim, 1965). By contrast the approach in Britain has been less structured, although there are a variety of educational resources including the Open University, a number of local voluntary initiatives and state provision such as the health visiting service, therapeutic day nurseries and various parents' groups run by social services departments.

Help with the new-born baby

Mention was made in Chapter 1 of the concept of bonding. Clearly there is a process which enables parents to respond to the needs of 'tiny infants who at first sleep for hours on end and only awaken to cry, eat, burp, soil, and fall asleep again' (Kennell *et al.*, 1976). Many parents feel an intense, almost painful love for their new-born babies. Others however feel very little at first but the love grows. In a few cases the parents report only feelings of aversion for their infants; in these cases bonding is said to have failed.

Sometimes a form of temporary mental illness can cause problems with the process of bonding. Daphne, a young mother developed a post-partum psychosis shortly after the birth of her first daughter. In the latter stages of her pregnancy she had been to see a film in which a baby was possessed by the devil. She believed her little girl was similarly possessed and she tried (unsuccessfully) to cut open the baby's stomach in order to 'let the devil out'. Medical treatment helped Daphne with her illness but, having recovered, she was left with negative feelings towards her daughter. She required counselling which was provided by a social worker. She was helped to appreciate that she was not responsible for her actions while ill and thus need not feel guilty. She was allowed to express her negative emotions and then helped to discover that she had some positive ones. Her feeling of revulsion turned to pity, which eventually turned to tenderness for her baby.

There is evidence that difficulties in the early post-partum, such as separation of mother from the baby have some relationship to bonding problems (Kennell *et al.*, 1976; Bolton, 1983). It is possible that the changes in maternity arrangements have helped to alleviate this. It was common practice in some hospitals for new-born babies to be taken to a nursery; the mothers were only 'allowed' to see their infants several hours later. Fathers were firmly excluded from the birth. Nowadays, in many hospitals fathers can choose to be present at the birth and parents and baby are left to spend time together immediately after the birth. Mothers can keep the baby in a cot by their bedside and are encouraged to breast-feed. This improved management helps parents to have a greater sense of belonging to, and being responsible for their infants.

There are a number of groups which help parents in difficulty with their new baby. In Britain these include 'MAMA (Meet-a-Mum Association)' which provides both practical and moral support for women suffering from postnatal depression or who are tired and isolated after the birth of a baby. Mothers suffering postnatal illness can also obtain advice from the 'Association for Postnatal Illness' which is run by mothers, backed up by medical experts, who have experienced this illness and have recovered. 'The National Childbirth Trust' gives genei help and support to parents before and after the birth.

Even when the parental bond is not strong parents can be taught how to react to their baby in a way which brings out the more delightful responses of an infant such as smiling and gurgling. In the Netherlands parents are helped in this way by the 'Body Language Foundation'. This organisation produces video films and other materials to help parents. The films cover topics such as birth, body contact in cases of prematurity and autistic children. One video demonstrates how a family can cope with a crying baby by, for example, talking to him in a high-pitched voice which elicits a more interested response from the infant than does a deep voice. Many parents and siblings naturally talk to the baby in a higher pitch than normal but some fail to realise the benefits of this.

Persistent crying can trigger an abusive response and a number of parents need help with this problem. Some simply do not realise their small baby can cry lustily when he is tired. They will continue to pick him up, try feeding and winding him only to make matters worse. They do not know that he needs to be settled, rocked, sung a lullaby or left with a tape of 'womb music' running. On the other hand some parents are persuaded not to pick their baby up for fear of 'spoiling' him. However if a tiny infant cries for more than a few minutes he is likely to need attention. It is impossible to 'spoil' a baby of a few weeks old and the only result of leaving him to cry for long periods is an agitated, fractious infant or an apathetic, unrewarding one. Sometimes crying is due to pain such as that resulting from an ear infection. Parents need help and advice to understand these factors. They should not be left to struggle on their own, only to feel more and more inadequate. Midwives and health visitors are often a source of assistance, while doctors can ensure there is no medical reason for persistent crying. Parents can also be encouraged to contact self-help groups such as 'Crysis' an organisation in Britain which assists parents with this problem.

Telephone help-lines

The beneficial nature of telephone help-lines has been recognised for many years, certainly since the 1950s when the Samaritans were founded in Britain by Chad Vara. Incidents of abuse sometimes occur because parents who are under stress have no one to turn to. When this was realised several telephone help-lines designed to assist them were set up. 'Parents Anonymous' is the name of one such help-line.

Counsellors will listen to the problems of each caller and will give individual guidance over the telephone. Some help-lines provide a back-up service; parents needing more than telephone contact will be visited by volunteers or invited to come into a centre for coffee and a chat.

There are a number of telephone services which have recorded messages giving advice on a wide variety of topics some of which relate to child abuse. In Britain there is the 'Parents Advice Line' which provides guidance on child care matters including 'Help for Parents Under Stress' who think they may hit or hurt their child. Another telephone service 'Healthcall' answers many medically related questions covering topics as diverse as skin cancer, vasectomy and AIDS but also includes incest and non-accidental injury to children. The merit of such services is that it takes very little courage to ring because callers do not have to speak or find the words to explain their predicament. The drawback is that the message cannot be tailored to individual needs, but at least hearing that your problem is acknowledged and you are not the only parent who feels like losing control is a help.

In a number of countries there are telephone help-lines for children who are being abused. In Britain ChildLine was set up in 1986 after a BBC television programme survey revealed the alarming extent of child abuse throughout the country. The telephones are manned mostly by a professional group of counsellors headed by a Director. The cost of the calls is borne by ChildLine and the children using the service do not have to give their names and addresses.

Not all the children ringing in will have been abused. For example one little girl rang for advice because she had stolen a birthday present for her grandmother from a shop. Her grandmother had been so delighted at her grand-daughter's generosity that the girl felt very guilty about what she had done. Some youngsters ring as a joke but usually the counsellors can detect the hoaxers; giggling can often be heard in the background. A handful of young people tell stories which are evident fabrications but which indicate a considerable degree of distress. Very many accounts of abuse are obviously genuine. Some callers refuse to give personal details because they do not want to cause trouble for the perpetrator or their family. But they welcome the opportunity to share their experiences with someone who understands their situation; it helps them to feel less isolated. Other callers can be persuaded to give details and allow the matter to be investigated by their local welfare agencies.

ChildLine is not designed to assist adults who were abused as children. There is, however, a need for such a service because many adults are still carrying the burden of their childhood abuse. Some forget their experiences for a while only to recall them when memories are triggered perhaps by a television programme. The 'flashbacks' and reawakening of long repressed emotions can be such a powerful experience that the former victim may become profoundly distressed. There are a number of help-lines for adults who were abused as children including 'Incest Survivors' lines.

Home-Start

Home-Start was founded in 1974 in Leicester, England by Margaret Harrison who was at the time a voluntary work organiser. The scheme uses volunteers who are themselves mothers. They befriend other mothers who are having difficulties with pre-school children, visiting them in their homes. The ultimate objective is to help the children learn and develop their potential and lead a fuller, happier life. This however is achieved through the parent who is viewed by Home-Start as the child's 'sustaining agent' and in the home which is seen as the 'sustaining background'. Though the focus is on the parent rather than the child, it is the child who is the ultimate beneficiary.

There is good evidence that Home-Start effects positive change in families (van der Eyken, 1982). It takes a variety of referrals but certainly some include situations thought to be potential child abuse cases. In its first four years Home-Start worked with 303 families of which 25 per cent were on the Leicester child abuse At Risk register. Environmental stress can contribute to parents losing control and injuring or neglecting their offspring. Home-Start volunteers help parents to cope with these stresses and may well prevent a serious loss of control.

Daphne, whom we met earlier in this chapter in the section on bonding, had a crisis of confidence when her daughter started school. She had just separated from her husband and was having difficulty coping with officials from social security, the gas and electricity boards and the housing department. She was then greeted by an aggressive, critical school teacher. Daphne was a naturally shy young woman who was unable to read or write easily and was readily intimidated. She began to doubt her ability as a mother. She felt that she could not cope and became depressed and impatient. She was allocated a Home-Start volunteer who helped her with her literacy problem and took her to the various officials showing her how to assert herself. Through this Daphne gained both the money and the consideration to which she was entitled. Given guidance by the volunteer she was also able to ignore or counter the criticisms of the teacher.

Potential volunteers have to participate fully in a training course. Those unable to commit themselves to the course will drop out at this stage. Each volunteer will tailor her intervention to the needs of a particular family. They have the support of a Home-Start organiser. In addition each Home-Start group has a multidisciplinary Support Group. One important feature is that Home-Start exploits local resources such as a Red Cross toy library.

Home-Start launched another scheme in Nottingham in 1978. Within ten years it had expanded into many areas throughout Britain and has now spread abroad. Maybe sometime in the future there would be scope for the befriending of families by families. Not only could mothers help other mothers but fathers assist fathers. The paternal role is increasingly recognised as important. It could be argued that many men would be more effective as fathers once they had gained confidence in their role.

Portage

Portage originated in the town of that name in America. It is based on the belief that the most appropriate people to teach skills to young children are their own parents. Everyone needs to acquire a variety of physical, emotional and social skills and most children learn them naturally from their parents or carers. However some parents and children need special help. Portage is a scheme most commonly used with children who have developmental difficulties due to physical or mental handicap. But other children may suffer impairment because their parents do not know how to provide proper stimulation. They may be neglected or be subjected to such unrealistic expectations and rigid discipline that they cannot explore their world freely or learn through trial and error.

In many cases such parents appreciate that they are having difficulties coping with the developmental demands of their young children. A Portage helper or visitor works with the parents and decides weekly and longer-term targets. The helper takes account of the parents' abilities as well as the child's capabilities. Tasks can vary from the social such as saying 'Thank you' to use of motor skills such as managing to put one toy brick on top of another. But as each task is set both parent and helper agree that it is an appropriate one for the particular child. They are guided by the helper's knowledge and training and by Portage Charts.

Portage was used successfully with a young mother, Kerstin, coping alone with a toddler. She was of limited intelligence and had been neglected as a child. She was nevertheless concerned about her son, Jason and was willing to accept help and guidance. Jason was showing poor weight gain and developmental delay. For a while Kerstin attended a Teenage Parents Group where staff felt she lacked confidence and had a poor self-esteem. She seemed unable to recognise and adapt to Jason's changing needs. A programme was drawn up part of which involved giving direct help to Kerstin such as teaching her to prepare meals, budget and maintain acceptable standards of hygiene. The other part of the programme was the use of Portage to help her respond to Jason's needs.

Within two months the team of workers identified positive changes. Kerstin's confidence was growing and she was delighted by the way Jason managed tasks through her own guidance. Jason in turn responded well to the attention he was now receiving from his mother. She began to acknowledge that she had some very positive attributes. Jason may well have developed as well had he been placed in a special nursery or given individual sessions with a specialist worker. But his progress would then only have served to reinforce Kerstin's feeling of inadequacy and failure, which could in turn have led to a deterioration in her relationship with her son.

Kidscape

There are a number of schemes, video tapes and teaching packages designed to help children protect themselves against sexual exploitation. Many of these focus on the danger from strangers. One drawback of the 'danger stranger' campaigns is that youngsters are given the impression that a stranger will look 'strange', i.e. ugly or odd. A child asked if someone who is clean, good-looking and knows their name is a stranger may well say 'no'. Unfortunately the fashion for children to wear personalised bracelets, badges, tee-shirts or bags increases the likelihood that a potential molester will learn their name. A second drawback is that children who are molested may not tell anyone because they feel guilty for having disobeyed, however unwittingly, the 'don't talk to strangers' injunction. Furthermore, it is now appreciated that a considerable number of children are molested not by strangers but by people whom they know, including siblings and parents.

'Kidscape Good Sense Defense Programme' for children avoids some of the pitfalls outlined above. It was founded by Michelle Elliot and Wendy Titman in 1986. Its objective is to help children recognise and cope with a variety of dangerous situations including ones which may give rise to sexual abuse. In the words of one of its founders 'The programme teaches children to trust their own feelings in sensing dangerous situations; to differentiate between safe and unsafe forms of touching; to break rules when necessary in order to protect themselves and always to seek adult help' (Elliott, 1986).

The programme involves children directly in role-play, question-and-answer sessions and discussions based on questionnaires. There is a kit which includes drawing and colouring exercises. The children are usually reached through sessions held in schools. Before a session with the pupils the co-operation of parents and teachers is gained and they are made aware of the content of the programme. This gives them the right and the opportunity to raise objections. Experience has shown that there are very few who oppose the scheme, which has proved remarkably popular and successful.

The programme begins with a number of general rules such as what the child should do if he or she becomes lost, how to make an emergency phone call and the importance of children telling their parents where they are going. One of its features is that it emphasises that children have certain rights including the right to be safe. This is important because children do not always know what minimum standards to expect; for example Mary, a twelve-year-old, rang ChildLine, 'Her voice was timid and tinged with sadness. In a very quiet voice Mary said, "I don't know whether I should phone you or not but I've been sleeping in an outside garage since I was two and my friends say that it is not right" ' (Griffiths, 1987). Evidently Mary was not being given basic care and protection at night but it took her ten years to begin to realise something might be amiss. The Kidscape programme also teaches children that they have a right to say 'no' if someone touches them in a way that frightens or confuses them.

The youngsters are helped to deal with bullies as well as potential molesters. They are encouraged to practice a yell which is deeper than a scream and can be produced even when fear takes over. Running away if possible is seen as one strategy but telling adults and not keeping secrets about being bullied or molested is emphasised. This ensures that if children find they are tricked or trapped they know that disclosure is the right course for them to take.

Finally although the Kidscape programme covers not talking to strangers it clarifies the nature of potential molesters and helps children recognise tricks or pressure that might be applied. It also helps youngsters appreciate that they have a right not to be abused by anyone, even if the perpetrator is someone they know and love.

Economic and social factors

The accounts by Marie, Helen and Sarah all demonstrate that child abuse in a variety of forms is not the sole province of poverty-stricken, socially deprived parents. Nevertheless there is reason to believe that the environment in which families live can contribute to abuse. Improvements in environmental conditions may therefore prevent some cases of child abuse. In addition there are social factors such as views on the status of children which influence all income groups and which can contribute to child abuse. A fundamental change in social attitudes could eradicate a significant proportion of abuse cases.

The exact part played by social, political and economic factors in relation to child abuse is a complex issue which has been the subject of considerable debate (e.g. Pelton, 1981; Parton, 1985). This section can therefore examine only a few of the many economic and social factors which may give rise to abuse and which if changed could prevent some of the mistreatment of children.

Housing and financial problems

The various environmental problems encountered by some parents is illustrated by the case of Becky, a single mother with a baby daughter. She lived on the fifth floor in a tower block complex in a large city in Britain. The walls of the flats were thin and life was generally noisy for the residents. The complex was depressing; a grey, rabbit-warren filthy with litter and excrement. The flats were damp and the community heating scheme provided only erratic heating. Although Becky lived on State support she had to hand over her money to a local 'protection' gang. She was then given back a small sum which enabled her to buy food. Consequently she was beset by financial problems but was occasionally helped by her mother. Sometimes she paid her own way by prostitution, an occupation which she disliked and which made her feel in her own words 'dirty and defiled'.

Becky's physical care of her daughter was good and despite having to hand-wash clothes the baby was usually clean. However, when the infant was only a few months old, Becky broke her daughter's arm. She admitted that she could not cope. Her social worker felt that, basically, Becky was a caring, capable woman and he tried to improve environmental conditions but the child, at Becky's insistence, had to be removed. A year later her second baby died, a victim of the sudden infant death syndrome; Becky was still living in the complex. By the time her third baby was born she had been moved to a house on a well-planned estate. She was far away from the protection gang, the damp, the erratic heating, the noise, the dirt and depression of the complex. Her third child has developed properly and has not been abused. Becky herself is more relaxed and confident in her new setting.

She was by no means the only parent in the complex to injure a child. Many families living there were known to the child protection agencies in the locality. The council eventually decreed that all families should be moved out. The conditions remained intolerable for the remaining residents and the complex was demolished.

It is acknowledged that poor living conditions generate additional stresses which may result in a parent's failure to cope when in better circumstances he or she would manage. In an analysis of 6532 cases Sue Creighton found that bad housing was a significant stress factor in 16 per cent of the cases (Creighton, 1984, p. 18). It is not only the noise, dirt, lack of safe play space, overcrowding and other physical problems that cause stress but also less tangible factors such as the low self-esteem created by the adverse reaction of other people to certain addresses.

Sue Creighton also found in the same study that financial problems were significant in about a third of the families. Overall the average income was lower than the national figures for earnings of manual workers. Unemployment of the head of the household was as high as 53.1 per cent in 1982, considerably higher than the national figures. Research by Gil conducted in the United States found that physical abuse, especially serious incidents, were overconcentrated among the poor (Gil, 1970, pp. 138–9).

The poor may be over-represented because they, more than the wealthy, are likely to come to the notice of the welfare agencies. They have fewer opportunities to escape difficult situations and cannot pay to have their children cared for by others. But above all there is the loss of self-worth, the humiliation and the frustration of powerlessness which goes hand in hand with poverty in those societies which tend to value people in terms of personal wealth. Gil (1970) argues that a change in housing policy and city planning would help prevent child abuse as would greater welfare provision for families. A less competitive more co-operative societal value system might result in a drop in the incidence of certain abuse cases, especially those of serious physical mistreatment.

Increased wealth on its own, however, will not result in the eradication of child abuse. In the Nordic countries standards of living are relatively high and economic factors are less significant in child care problems that they used to be. Family violence, psychiatric illness and alcohol or drug abuse have featured more in the child welfare statistics in the past 10–20 years. Child abuse still exists, 'This may be the result of a more complicated society or another selection of child welfare clients' (Grinde, 1987). Even fatalities due to abuse occur in relatively affluent families. The Inquiry into the death of Christopher Pinder, adopted and called Daniel Frankland (1981), noted that the adoptive parents at whose hands Daniel died had a lifestyle which created 'favourable impressions' (Pinder/Frankland, 1981, p.7).

Attitudes to children and child rearing

Valerie Yule watched the behaviour of adults with children in public and found that while adults were usually courteous to other adults there was widespread rudeness towards children (Yule, 1985). This reflects a general, underlying negative attitude towards children which may lead many parents towards abusive behaviour. A more positive view of youngsters would make a lot of mistreatment unacceptable and would prevent many cases escalating into ones of serious abuse.

In many countries this negative attitude towards children pervades society. They are regarded as a nuisance to the extent that, for example, only a handful of restaurants in Britain cater for youngsters despite the fact that those which target young customers make healthy profits. Very little provision is made for push-chairs, especially double ones, in city centres. Children's clothes departments are invariably in the most inaccessible place in department stores. Mothers have to breast-feed their babies in toilets when they are out and about unless they are able to disregard disapproving stares and unpleasant comments. This all reflects a society which does not value children and makes few attempts to meet their needs.

Children as parental property – children are people who happen to be young in years. They cannot be another person's property just as one adult cannot be the property of another in those societies which have abolished slavery. Children are people in the care of another until they can care for themselves. The carer has no right to harm them whatever his or her beliefs about the correct way to behave. This is a simple philosophy but not one reflected in many societies. The smaller the child the more he or she is regarded as parental property.

Babies, especially the unborn, are particularly vulnerable because a mother's right to do as she wants is supported over and above possible risks to the baby's health and future welfare. It is known that alcohol, cigarette and other drug consumption and certain infections can have an adverse effect on unborn or breast-fed infants, yet in few countries are restrictions placed on pregnant women or nursing mothers. This attitude is reflected in a DHSS report (1988). In relation to breastfeeding and AIDS the report stated,

> A proportion of mothers who are HIV seropositive in pregnancy will transmit the virus to the fetus in utero, and infection has been transmitted by breastfeeding . . . as a means of reducing the risk to the baby to a minimum , HIV seropositive mothers in the UK should be discouraged from breastfeeding. However, where a mother insists on breastfeeding it is her right to be assisted to do so (DHSS, 1988, p. 18).

This statement totally disregards the newly-born person's right to good health. Parents often know what is best for their children and parental rights are to be respected. But in cases where parents fail to protect their offspring society has a duty to take over the protective function.

Children's rights – the recognition that children can have rights independent of their parents is beginning to emerge, although as the preceding section demonstrates there is an ambivient attitude to these. Many cases of child abuse could be prevented if children were given clear and inalienable rights, equivalent as far as possible to the rights given to adults. This idea appears to cause consternation. For example, in Britain the principle of parental attendance at case conferences has been generally accepted, whereas the idea of including children has been met with reservations (see 'Mixed response to children in case conference idea', *Social Work Today*, Vol. 20, no. 1, p. 2). Yet the objections in the case of both parents and children are similar. Care will have to be taken not to cause undue distress to either parent or child and the confidences of third parties have to be maintained. But these difficulties could be overcome given the will to respect the rights of children.

The acknowledgement that children have rights does not, however, mean that they should be treated exactly like adults or have the same range of responsibilities. One area in which they are expected to cope with adult conditions is in the English courts. Yet this is inappropriate because they are handicapped in their ability to communicate and comprehend due to their developmental limitations. A blind person would not be expected to pick out an offender in a visual identity parade, a Frenchman with only a few English phrases would be allowed a translator in court. Provisions are made by many legal systems for adults who are restricted in some way, yet in England and in many other countries this principle is not extended to children.

Corporal punishment – 'The single most important determinant of child abuse is the willingness of adults to inflict corporal punishment upon children in the name of discipline. Well over half of all instances of abuse appear to have developed out of disciplinary action' (Zigler, 1979, p. 40). Many societies accept violence towards children in the name of punishment. Discipline should not however be equated with violence. The cat-o'-nine tails and keel-hauling is no longer seen as necessary to the maintenance of discipline in the Royal Navy; objections are now raised against keeping women or employees in order through the use of the stick or belt; dog owners are now encouraged to train their animals by reward, praise and tone of voice rather than by use of the whip. Yet this enlightenment does not seem to have filtered down to the discipline of children. Parents and, in some areas, teachers are still permitted to beat children to the point of injury with a variety of implements.

The training of children is much influenced by a society's traditions and culture. Although these should be respected, closer examination often shows that adults interpret aspects of their culture to meet their own needs. For example, the Judeo/Christian tradition appears to advocate corporal punishment because of various Old Testament injunctions summarised by the satirist Samuel Butler (1612–80) in his phrase 'Spare the rod and spoil the child'. However many parents following the Judeo/Christian tradition who oppose corporal punishment will point to the Good Shepherd of the 23rd Psalm and the New Testament who has a rod to guide sheep who may be straying and to fend off any threats to his herd. Thus, they argue, parents will spoil a child if they do not provide guidance, protection and sensible boundaries but just as beating sheep is pointless so beating children is unnecessary and counter-productive.

It is clear that many children are seriously injured or killed because their parents believe in corporal punishment and society endorses that belief. Lisa Godfrey (1975) was killed by a mother irritated by the three-year-old girl's bed-wetting and behaviour which made the mother feel that, as recorded in the Inquiry report, 'the child provoked her to lose her temper and to hit her' (Godfrey, 1975, p. 6). Wayne Brewer (1977) was killed by a step-father who hit him because in his words, 'Some things he says just annoys me' (Brewer, 1977, p. 18). Charles Courtney who killed Darryn Clarke (1979) began, as noted in the Inquiry report, 'to exercise what he may have regarded as a father's rights over the child and to enforce a harsh form of discipline' (Clarke, 1979, p. 11). It would seem that a proportion of abuse cases would be prevented if the most dangerous forms of chastisement were clearly prohibited such as hitting babies, involving the head area, using fists or instruments and punishing in any way that resulted in injury.

8

The Effects of Abuse – the Later Years

This chapter looks at the prospects for abused children in later life. The first section examines some of the evidence that exists about the long-term effects of abuse. This is followed by accounts of the early adulthood and present situations of Marie, Helen and Sarah. Their updated stories are retold in the third person because by this means objective observations can be made. The final section examines ways in which social workers can help adults who were abused as children.

Evidence of long-term effects

There have been a number of research studies which attempt to show the long-term effects of abuse on children. There are, however, difficulties in collecting and interpreting data which may, if discounted, give rise to faulty assumptions.

Methodological considerations

One way of determining the long-term effects of childhood abuse is to assess adults who were mistreated as children then compare them with others who were not. Unfortunately researchers usually have to rely on the subjective assessment of the participants to determine who was and who was not abused. A social worker, for example, took a history from a client who declared she had good although strict parents who only 'tapped' her when she deserved punishment. Records revealed that she had been injured by her father's severe beatings on a number of occasions. With the passage of time abuse can be seen as a minor problem or justifiable chastisement, sometimes adults simply forget what happened; in all these instances they will deny having been abused.

Conversely a few adults who would not normally be regarded as abused as children maintain that they were in order to gain sympathy or because they resented aspects of their parents' behaviour. A man who had molested a number of young girls stated that he did so because he had been sexually abused as a child. When asked about specific incidents he explained that as an army recruit, aged eighteen, he had been 'touched up' by his sergeant major. Although this was a distressing incident for a young man, which may have had a bearing on his subsequent behaviour, it would not usually be regarded as 'child abuse'.

There is a similar problem over choosing a reliable control group in studies which involve selecting a number of abused children and assessing them over time. Certainly Helen and Sarah could have found themselves in a control group of apparently non-abused children with which the group of abused children would have been matched and compared.

Another problem with longitudinal studies is the problem of keeping in contact with the selected children. Lynch and Roberts noted:

> When reviewing the literature we were alarmed by the number of children in other researchers' original samples that were unavailable for follow-up assessment. . . . Obviously results which reflect the assessments of less than half the original samples are open to serious criticism as there could be an enormous difference between those families who attend for follow-up assessment and those who do not . . . some of the lost children could be dead. (Lynch and Roberts, 1982, p.4)

It is also difficult to determine which factors are attributable to the abuse and which to other influences such as peer group pressures, changing schools and accidents. Some features such a mental handicap which appear to be a result of abuse may have existed undetected prior to any mistreatment.

Negative consequences

For a number of children death is the ultimate negative consequence. For other children there is the burden of severe handicap. One baby, Michelle, was sixteen days old when she was picked up by the feet by her father and her head smashed against the floor. She was rushed to a specialist hospital and her life saved. However, two years later she was severely mentally and physically handicapped only able to make a small range of noises and unable to control her body. She was living in a children's home and there were doubts about the possibility of finding a foster home for her.

Other children have to live with disfiguring scars from cuts, burns and scalding. But many more have emotional scars which do not show so readily. Helen described how, when her memories came flooding back, she felt as if she had open wounds rubbed raw by every remembered detail and by the insensitive remarks of well-meaning acquaintances. Gradually her wounds healed although small scars remained.

Emotional and behavioural difficulties which have been recorded in follow-up studies of abused children include lack of confidence, depression and hostility (Lynch and Roberts, 1982), aggression (Reidy, 1977; Wolfe, 1987), self-destructive behaviour (Green, 1978) and deficits in academic performance, social sensitivity and moral judgements (Wolfe, 1987). Many adult former victims mourn the loss of their childhood and they therefore share characteristics, including depression, guilt and anger, usually associated with people who have suffered bereavements and have an unresolved grief reaction. Physically abused and neglected children often show developmental and intellectual delay especially in relation to language and verbal performance (Lynch and Roberts, 1982).

In relation to sexual abuse, eating disorders and psychiatric problems have been noted as well as 'feelings of rejection, guilt, unworthiness, inability to cope with normal sexual relationships and a general distrust of helping agencies' (Oppenheimer, 1985, p. 27). In a comprehensive study of the long-term effects of child sexual abuse Beezley and Mrazek (1981) list 25 problem areas ranging from aversion to sexual activity and problems with parents or in-laws to masochism and murder.

One of the consequences of abuse which gives rise to considerable concern is the evidence of a cycle of abuse from one generation to the next. Chapter 1 demonstrated that sometimes abuse victims interpret parental behaviour as strong, courageous and justified, a model which they grow up to emulate. 'In addition to providing models which can be imitated families, through their use of violence, teach that violence is an acceptable form of expression or problem solving' (Gelles and Strauss, 1979, p. 542). Children who have been neglected may never have been shown how to run a clean, efficient household when they reach adulthood. Sexual abuse victims may protect their self-image by convincing themselves that there is nothing wrong in sexual relationships between adults and children and may indulge in such activities themselves or ignore the abuse of their own children by another adult.

Certain abused children may grow up to wreak havoc in society. For example, writing of those men who raped children and can be described as fixated paedophiles Ray Wyre comments, 'Many men in this category have been sexually abused as children and have incorporated their abuse experiences into their own sexuality' (Wyre,

1986). Andrew, a prisoner serving four life sentences commented, 'I didn't like my dad, he was too fond of the belt. He was always laying into me with his belt' (Parker, 1969, p. 205).

Some people abused as children become so trapped in their situation that they literally have to blast their way out. Often quiet, introverted people, they collect guns and other weapons as a means of giving them the power and control they had so desperately needed as vulnerable, mistreated children. Then comes the day when they use the weapons to make their bid for freedom turning them against their family, any innocent passers-by and finally themselves.

It perhaps comes as no suprise that Hitler's father was:

'a drunkard and a tyrant . . . in Hitler's case the love for his young mother and the hate for his old father assumed morbid proportions . . . which drove him to love and to hate and compelled him to save or destroy people and peoples who really "stand for" his mother and his father". (Erikson, 1965, pp. 319–20)

Children who do well

By no means all abused children end up as child rapists, mass murderers or sadistic tyrants. Although some may have social difficulties and private sorrows others may grow-up to be happy, well-adjusted individuals who provide excellent care for their own offspring.

In their examination of the long-term effects of child sexual abuse Beezley and Mrazek (1981) cite four studies which found no ill-effects in adulthood. In a follow-up study of abused children and their siblings Lynch and Roberts (1982) noted that 37 per cent (23 per cent abused and 51 per cent siblings) appeared to have no particular problems, they could enjoy themselves and were self-confident. They were also healthy, neurologically intact, well grown, intellectually normal and had no discernible behaviour disturbances. They could form good relationships with both adults and children.

Lynch and Roberts went on to identify a number of factors which may contribute to a positive outlook for abused children. Absence of perinatal problems and early intervention, before any developmental and behavioural problems came to the force, were important. Although many youngsters were the subjects of legal proceedings these were not protracted or recurrent and placement changes were few. High intelligence was identified as a possible protective factor. Siblings who seemed to do well were those who were born after the identification of abuse which adds weight to the view that witnessing abuse can be as damaging as being the recipient – the only true non-abused siblings are those who are not in the household during the period of abuse. Probably the most important factor is that the children who did well had successfully completed the first development stage and had been able to establish basic trust in themselves and in other people (see Erikson, 1965). This enabled them to establish good relationships and these in turn reinforced the children's sense of autonomy and of being valued.

It seems that if adults make the effort to love and value abused children they may be able to help establish or restore the youngsters' sense of self-worth. Lynch and Roberts mention a number of different people who were able to help the victims of abuse in this way – long-term foster parents, a care centre staff member and a father determined to make up for his wife's inability to look after their son.

However there is evidence that even as adults victims can be helped, despite having been repeatedly abused as children and despite having no consistent caring figure for much of their early life. Phil Quinn found 'salvation' in the form of acceptance by a group of motor-bikers 'Satan's Saints' (Quinn, 1988) and Tom O'Neill met unstinting care, which gave him a sense of being valued, by the staff of a probation hostel (O'Neill, 1981). In the following accounts it will be seen that Marie, Helen and Sarah were all given significant help in their adult lives.

Marie's account continued

Marie was married early to a man who was violent and sexually abusive. She returned to her parent's home only to be molested by her father. She realised how inappropriate her father's attitude to his children was when on one occasion during this period he was trying to kiss her, using considerable force. As Marie resisted he shouted, 'What's the matter? You're a woman and I'm a man'. Marie responded with, 'No, you're my father and I'm your daughter'.

While back with her parents Marie formed a relationship with Rob, a young friend of her father. He was gentle and trustworthy, never showing any anger or swearing. He felt that he was sexually impotent so theirs was a platonic friendship. Marie was able to receive a cuddle from him without feeling dirty and defiled. Rob showed her that not all men were violent and demanding like her father and her first husband.

Rob was sensitive and observant. He could judge Marie's mood from the clothes she chose to put on. If she was in a long dress then he would treat her as a lady, if she was in a mini-skirt he would flirt with her. But she always felt safe with him. Occasionally her mood would alter during the evening and he would patiently return home with her so that she could change her clothes.

Marie liked Rob but never loved him. After a while she was able to move on to a relationship which demanded more commitment. Her second husband, Luke was gentle and caring like Rob; but she loved him, found him physically attractive and was able to have a satisfactory sexual relationship with him. Rob remained in the background for a while and told her, 'I'll always be in the bank for you emotionally'. Marie realised that she was now strong enough to help her husband when he needed support.

The couple had a number of children and when one child was molested Marie immediately sought help for her youngster. It is important to emphasise that neither parent was responsible for the incident. Furthermore their child was able to tell them what had happened and they went to great lengths to ensure that all their children were protected in future. The events were distressing for all the family but especially for Marie who not only felt that in some way she must be to blame but also had to bear again the pain of knowing that a family member was abused, just as when she was a child she suffered because of the misery inflicted on her mother and siblings.

At the time, Marie was attending a self-help group for adults who had been abused as children. She found that the support of its members was important to her and they helped her put events into perspective. She also received help during this critical period from a very gentle, caring male social worker who referred her to a psychotherapist. She benefited from the counselling she was given but did not need such intensive help for long. Eventually, she became a 'senior member' of the self-help group giving assistance to newer members who were at a more vulnerable and painful stage of the healing process.

Marie views her father with a mixture of anger and pity. He is an old man now. When the family visits her parents she ensures that none of her children are left alone with him. Pauline, her elder sister, still has emotional difficulties and cannot communicate with her husband; she will attack him even if he has only one drink. Linda married a violent man who broke her arm and then found solace in relationships with women. Marie's brother, Barry, followed their father into the Services but he was convicted of causing grievous bodily harm and given a dishonorable discharge. He is still very violent and in Marie's words 'mixed up and not coping with adult life'.

Marie herself is still sometimes affected by her experiences. She acknowledges that she is a 'worrier'. She 'worries for others' and becomes anxious about potential problems before they arrive.

Nevertheless she is determined that her father, having destroyed her childhood, will not destroy her future. She is a tall, elegant woman who dresses smartly and has an air of confidence mixed with a warm, generous manner. Asked what helped her survive those unhappy earlier years Marie replied that humour had been her salvation, she would always try to see the funny side of any situation.

Helen's account continued

During her teenage years Helen concentrated on her academic studies. She wanted to be a doctor but always doubted her ability to achieve this goal and could not believe that a medical school would give her a place. She was frightened of failure. She therefore opted for a career in nursing. Her eating problems meant that although she found the academic work relatively easy the physical demands of the job nearly defeated her as she had so litle stamina. Eventually she managed to complete her training.

During her time as a student nurse she met Hugh. He worked at the nearby university. He was an academic involved in research. He was an idealist committed to fund-raising for Third World countries. He expressed love for Helen, who now believes that her half-starved, tired appearance appealed to his belief in an ascetic way of life; he rejected any form of indulgence or luxury. Helen became engaged to Hugh. He made no sexual demands which suited her; he said they would wait until they were married. However, Helen began to find that his coldness, his inability to cuddle her or express any deep affection and his growing criticisms were a reminder of her mother's way of relating to her. Despite the fact that she was drawn to him like a magnet she refused to go with him when he moved to a new job at another university. The engagement was over and Helen was left feeling very lonely but certain that she had made the right decision.

Years passed and Helen became a health visitor. She developed an interest in child neglect. Although contented in her work she continued to have a bleak time as far as her personal life was concerned. She was unable to relate sexually to any partner and was frequently informed by a string of disenchanted, scornful men that she was 'frigid'.

She then met Jack. In contrast to Hugh he was outgoing, fun to be with and enjoyed the luxuries of life. He was physically attractive. He helped Helen feel that she too could be attractive. She felt able to put on a little weight and buy fashionable clothes. He was an adept lover and gently re-introduced her to sexual intercourse. For the first time in her life she enjoyed a sexual relationship. She married him but shortly after the wedding discovered that he had already been married two times before. She also found that he was an unreliable spendthrift with a fearsome temper. His sexual demands became more than she could tolerate. One day he walked out and the marriage, somewhat to Helen's relief, was over.

Shortly after this Helen began to recall the sexual abuse of her childhood. She had more or less forgotten about Frank's activities. Suddenly night after night and day after day memories came flooding back. Then she started crying and continued to cry whenever she was alone. Occasionally she did so when she was in company and then she had to pretend she had a cold or an eye infection. She eventually told a colleague who tried at first to help her but who then began to be intolerant of her moods swings. This made Helen feel even more unwanted, unworthy, a useless person who had a dreary past and a bleak, lonely future. She could see no good reason for not committing suicide.

Then from somewhere came a small voice which said that she was worth helping. She sought the help of a female counsellor who did much to restore her self-esteem. She was also given psychotherapy by a male therapist. He helped her to make connections between her experiences, her behaviour and her relationships. She went through a period of extreme anger and bitterness, but at the same time she began to value her own positive features.

Later Helen met Bill, a kindly, warm-hearted man who, like her father was involved in business. She had no problems relating to him sexually and they have produced a number of children. Helen is determined her children will have a mother who cuddles them, spends time with them and takes interest in what they are doing. Occasionally she finds herself copying her mother's off-hand manner and although she quickly checks this she has to be on constant guard against any seeming coldness especially when her children are ill. Nevertheless she is surprised how affectionate she is towards her offspring and how genuinely interested and concerned about them she is.

Reflecting on her ability to be a loving mother, Helen feels that she owes much to a neighbour, Mrs Stevens. As a teenager Helen used to visit the Stevens family and began to help with the care of the babies as each arrived. She was trusted to baby-sit and to take the youngsters for walks. Mrs Stevens was a warm, kindly lady who showed all her children physical affection. She provided a model for Helen who sometimes still finds herself copying Mrs Stevens' gestures and phrases.

Looking at Helen today she is an attractive woman with a buoyant self-esteem. There are however moments when her face looks sad and thoughtful. She is happy now but somehow feels that she does not deserve happiness, believing that one day it will all be taken away from her. On the other hand she recognises that the sense of being undeserving is a legacy of her childhood. So she continues to struggle against the feeling of impending disaster and tries to replace it with an optimistic view of the future.

Sarah's account continued

Having left home, Sarah went to live with her aunt and uncle until she felt ready for greater independence. They did not try to stop her leaving, they appreciated the fact that she needed to move on. Living in digs she met a woman who accepted her and hearing of her experiences commented, 'It isn't fair, why should it have happened to you'. This helped Sarah realise that she was not to blame for what had occurred and there was nothing bad about her, she did not deserve such treatment. She learnt about friendship from that woman and was able through her to make other friends. Sarah explained, 'I reached out a little, it worked so I reached out a little further'.

Sarah then married Mark a kindly, mild-mannered man. She acknowledges that she almost married a man like her father in the form of the boyfriend to whom she became engaged when she was seventeen. She realised when she had recovered from the broken engagement that she did not want to marry a bully. Mark is very similar to her grandfather who, as described by Sarah, was 'the one good man who could love in a giving way, who loved me for myself and who, with his wife, could offer me a safe family'. Sarah's grandparents also loved each other so she had faith in a loving relationship.

Sarah knows that it has taken her a long time to work through her feelings of worthlessness. She started the work herself. She raised her own family and completed a teacher training course. She reached a position of strength but recognised that she could become inappropriately angry. Furthermore, she would dwell on the deaths of people to whom she was close. She had a profound sense of loss and was stuck in the anger of that loss; in Sarah's words 'It was beginning to explode'. She knew the anger was inappropriate so she sought help from a counsellor.

She still had problems over body image and general worth. In therapy she recalled, amid intense pain, the incident when her father called her a 'pregnant cow'. The counsellor made her realise that what her father had shouted on the beach that day was untrue, emphasising, 'That was a lie, a vicious lie'. Sarah rejoiced in the realisation of the fact that her father was not always right and she was able to lay her burden of anger down.

Sarah also had to cope with a difficult period when a head of department, Mrs A, took a dislike to her and made her life a misery. Sarah realised that the woman felt threatened by her apparent strength and efficiency therefore she told Mrs A about her childhood in an attempt to demonstrate her vulnerablity. After this revelation Mrs A became increasingly vindictive. Perplexed, Sarah went to a colleague for help. The colleague observed that Mrs A was probably even more threatened now because she knew Sarah had the strength to survive such a testing childhood.

Despite the influence of Mrs A, Sarah's teaching abilities were recognised and she is now on the way to having a very successful career. Barbara lives abroad and there is still only a distant, superficial relationship between the two sisters. Their parents divorced and their father emigrated. Sarah has no contact with him. Her mother, while still married, tried to throw herslf out of a window, but once divorced could cope no better alone and turned more and more to drink. She eventually died and was lying dead for a fortnight before anyone found her body.

Sarah is a vivacious, attractive woman with a happy marriage, grown-up children, and a blossoming career. She can readily be described as a warm person with a bright, cheerful expression in her eyes. When asked what helped her survive she, like Marie, mentioned humour. She recalled how stupid her father looked having an erection in his dressing-gown. She has retained her sense of humour. Sarah also had a much loved dog and was able to escape the house by taking him for long walks. The countryside around was very beautiful and this sustained her. She felt the mountains belonged to her and used to 'fill up on the beauty of the mountains'. She found that she was and is creative with considerable artistic gifts. She managed to win a prize and knew that this was a talent her father could not deny her.

Sarah is now free of the burden of abuse. She once pointed to a photograph of herself as a little girl saying, 'How could my father have done that to me, I was a lovely child'. She is aware that some of the children she teaches are being abused. She is not sorry that she was abused because she can use her experiences to help others.

Helping adult survivors

The phrase 'adult survivor' is used in this section to refer to those abused children who reach independent adulthood. Not all do; some are killed, some commit suicide, some die of preventable diseases – sexually transmitted or as a result of neglect. Others are permanently damaged in such a way that, mentally and emotionally, they remain like dependent children.

As illustrated by the accounts of Marie, Helen and Sarah it is never too late to attempt to release an adult survivor from the negative feelings and inaccurate perspectives which imprison them. Men and women who were abused over fifty years ago have sought and received assistance. If an abused person is not helped during childhood he or she may have to live with a lot of pain, but no one should be condemned to life-long misery. Those involved in child welfare may well have skills which could also help 'grown-up' abused children.

Helping the individual

Adults sometimes carry a heavier burden than children because negative feelings arising from the abuse may have been reinforced over time. They will have an increased number of painful incidents to remember if, like Marie and Sarah, the abuse continued into their late teens or early twenties. One of the most constructive initial steps is to encourage the survivor to recall as much of his or her early life as possible. This is often a very painful process and may take several months especially when the person being helped has suppressed the most difficult incidents. Nevertheless it is in many cases a necessary journey. Having described events it is easier to view them from a more accurate perspective. Sarah describes how during counselling she was able to recognise that her father had lied about her. Having been relived and reassessed, such incidents can be left behind and the survivor can move on.

Anger needs to be dealt with. Often in the wake of recall comes long-suppressed anger. Frequently it is directed towards the survivor, him or herself. Sometimes it is targeted at society in general or a particular group in society such as men or authority figures like the police. Occasionally it is turned against the therapist – 'you can't know what it felt like'. 'I bet you are enjoying this, hearing the juicy details'. Survivors need to be helped to express anger against the perpetrators of the abuse and those who failed to protect them. They then need to move on to make sense of events, directing their anger into constructive rather than destructive channels. Anger made both Marie and Sarah determined that even though their fathers had ruined their childhoods they were not going to spoil their future. Anger has spurred people into helping abused children, setting-up schemes to prevent abuse or supporting other adults abused during childhood.

All survivors share a sense of loss. They have lost their only opportunity to be carefree, cared for children. They need to work through this loss in the same way that bereaved people have to complete the task of mourning. They, like those who are grieving, can be helped to come to terms with what has happened. They have to acknowledge that the loss has occurred, accept that they need not bear any guilt and express feelings, doubts and fears.

Survivors need to reach a stage when they can look back at themselves as children and can imagine cuddling and comforting their child-self. They must want to tell that child that he or she is lovable, was not to blame for the abuse and has nothing of which to be ashamed. One exercise which is useful, especially towards the end of individual work, involves the survivors finding a photograph of themselves when young. They look at this and describe how they feel about the child they see. Once the mourning and healing process is complete they will be able to express only positive emotions about their child-self. Some people will not have any childhood photographs; a drawing or a picture of child resembling them will do instead.

Group therapy

Groups for adult survivors can vary in form from relatively short-term projects run by professional workers to open-ended self-help groups. Adults, unlike children, can take on responsibility for running their own group. One model is that of a self-help group started by experienced group workers who are already skilled in assisting the victims of various situations. These 'facilitators' set up the group in response to a perceived demand. They make the initial practical arrangements such as finding meeting rooms and organising refreshments.

Facilitators also help in the healing process, preventing the group from becoming stuck in a mood of despair or destructive anger. As one or two survivors work through their problems they take over the responsibility for both practical arrangements and for assisting newer or more vulnerable members. Eventually the facilitators withdraw from group sessions, remaining in the background as advisers in case the members need guidance. Workers contemplating setting up such a self-help group should recognise that they will need to commit themselves for at least a year as facilitators and a further one or two years in an advisory capacity. There should be two facilitators and a consultant available to the group. However, once the facilitators have withdrawn it is possible for only one to remain involved as adviser.

The main benefit of group therapy is that it alleviates the sense of isolation that so many survivors experience. This is particularly important for sexually-abused men because much of the publicity is directed towards physical abuse and sexually victimised girls. Bruckner and Johnson who ran groups for such men write 'Male clients who were referred to the group had reached an impasse in their individual therapy. They continued to perceive sexual abuse as an experience unique to themselves. They viewed themselves as societal oddities, which in turn reinforced their guilt' (Bruckner and Johnson, 1987).

Group work always requires careful preparation. Facilitators need to think and talk through all the problems that they can anticipate. If they themselves were abused as children how will they respond when asked about their own experiences? Are they using the group as a therapeutic tool for themselves? If they were not abused how will they reply to the accusation of failing to understand what it is like to be abused? What action if any should the facilitators take if they learn that a member is now abusing a child? What will they do if a member appears to be suicidal?

As with children's groups it is important that several members should turn up for the first session. Again it is worth arranging for a few members to arrive together. Meetings should be held at least weekly. Often members will feel the need for more frequent contact and will meet together informally between sessions. Transport seems to be less of a problem than it is with children's groups because adults can often drive, manage to arrive by public transport or arrange to share a taxi. However, many potential members will have their own youngsters therefore a crèche may be necessary.

Activities can help to promote or direct discussion. However, adults, more than children, will tend to want to talk at length because they have much to talk about. Bruckner and Johnson (1987) recommend eliciting specific details of the abusive experiences at the outset. But there is a lot to be achieved in the first session including clarifying boundaries, agreeing on the purpose of the group and becoming familiar with members' names. It may therefore be more appropriate in the first session for members to introduce themselves with brief details of their experiences, for example, 'I'm Sarah and I've come because my father physically and sexually abused me' – leaving more detailed disclosures for later meetings.

There should be few rules but it is helpful if members agree to finish promptly. There is a tendency for people to put off bringing up difficult subjects till the last possible moment. This can place other members who have to leave on time in a dilemma. They may be unable to stay any longer but by going feel they have failed the distressed member. It should be clarified that if participants are to be helped then they must raise problems in good time. In a case of severe distress a facilitator may have to spend some time after the main session assisting the member with the immediate crisis and helping him or her bring it to the group on another occasion.

Although planned exercises will often have to be shelved because members want to talk it is sometimes worth applying gentle pressure to persuade the group to move on with the aid of an exercise. Tried and tested relaxation techniques can be practised and drawing is useful. At some stage members can be asked to draw what the abuse meant to them then, or perhaps at a later session, the perpetrator. This helps to focus discussion. Letters can be written to perpetrators, for sharing with other members rather than for posting.

Some members find both exercises and discussions difficult. They should not be made to feel embarrassed if they are unable to participate fully. If, for example, they cannot bring themselves to draw the perpetrator they can be invited to draw either a symbol or someone else that has upset them. It is often fellow members rather that the facilitators who give comfort to those in difficulty. However, the facilitators must be sensitive to the needs of different members – encouraging some to talk, allowing others to sit quietly and listen, discouraging some from going over and over events in a unproductive way and enabling others to repeat what they have said.

Final comment

Many social workers, other professionals and volunteers striving to help the victims of child abuse may wonder from time to time whether their intervention is effective. It is not unreasonable to assume that youngsters who have been exposed to years of mistreatment will need at least as many years of consistent affection and care in order to be released from the negative effects of abuse.

Nevertheless from the accounts given by Marie, Helen and Sarah it is clear that short-term intervention can create positive change in the courses of victims' lives. All three had, as adults, counselling, psychotherapy or the support of a self-help group. Furthermore, in their teenage years or early twenties they all had someone special to give them direct help. For Marie Rob, a caring male, opened her eyes to the fact that not all men are violent and demanding. She acknowledged that he gave her that which many male social workers give their clients, showing sensitivity and caring but not expecting any sexual favours. Mrs Stevens, Helen's model of someone who could accept her and who demonstrated how to show affection towards other children, can be found in foster parents, residential staff and in group leaders. Sarah's female friend whom she met in lodgings has her counterpart in those social workers who recognise the injustice of abuse and who prove trustworthy helpers.

Rob, Mrs Stevens and Sarah's friend were only involved with the three young women for a relatively short time and none were family members. Yet they all played a vital part in the lives of the three. They did much to undo the damage caused by close family members over many years. It is therefore quite possible that through properly focused individual, family or group work, assistance given by committed social workers will be effective in helping the victims of child abuse.

Guide to Further Reading

Full details of works cited are given in the bibliography.

Chapter 1 The Perspective of the Abused Child

Jones *et al.* (1987) is a comprehensive overview of the subject of child abuse while the concepts contained in this chapter are discussed more fully in Doyle (1985). A basic introduction to family theory is provided by Leslie (1982). Strenz (1980) gives a clear description of the Stockholm syndrome. A valuable explanation of the way in which sexually-abused children adapt to their situation can be found in Summit (1983). Useful insights into the perspective of distressed children are given in Bloch (1979).

Chapter 2 Voices of the Children

There are an increasing number of accounts by former victims of child abuse among these are: Angelou (1984), Cameronchild (1978) and Spring (1987). The work by Spring is the account of an incest survivor who witnessed the physical abuse of her brother and was eventually helped by a social worker. Pointers to recognising abuse in children are given in Stern (1987). Cooper (1985) lists worrying interactions and behaviour in young children. Indicators of child sexual abuse in boys are given in an article by Sebold (1987).

Chapter 3 Individual Work, with Children

Because work with abused children bears many similarities to work with bereaved children Jewett (1984) may prove useful. A collection of papers on various aspects of direct work with children is edited by Holgate (1972). Practical guidance on interviewing sexually-abused children is given by Jones and McQuiston (1985), Glaser and Frosh

(1988) and Vizard and Tranter (1988). A general description of play therapy is provided by Kezur (1981). Playwork with sexually-abused children is detailed in Doyle (1987). Games to help build up the relationship between worker and child can be found in The Catholic Children's Society publication (1983). Hindmann (1983) is written for children to help them understand they have a right not to be molested. An appealing 'facts of life' book has been written by Mayle (1973). Children can be helped to express themselves by using an unconventinal colouring book by Skinner and Kimmel (1984). The effects on some workers of involvement in sexual abuse cases is illustrated by Doyle (1986) while Narducci (1987) examines the issues for male workers dealing with such cases.

Chapter 4   Work With Children in the Family Context

Live supervision is presented in detail in Blakey *et al.* (1986). Family therapy in a clinical setting in child sexual abuse cases is discussed by Elton (1988). The work of one family centre is described by Adamson and Warren (1983) while Wratten (1985) examines both assessment and treatment based on the work of another family centre.

Chapter 5   Group Work with Abused Children

There is a growing number of articles on group work with sexually-abused children including Vizard (1987), Furniss *et al.* (1988) and Hildebrand (1988). A thoughtful account of group work with sexually-abused boys is given by Leith and Handforth (1988). Few descriptions of groups specifically for physically abused and neglected children have been written. There are a number of general books on group work with young people such as Konopka (1972) and Button (1974).

Chapter 6   Substitute Care

An overview of the issue of substitute care is given in the Report of the Working Party on Fostering Practice, DHSS (1976) and Thoburn (1988). Useful guides containing practical ideas for helping children in care are produced by the Association of British Adoption and Fostering Agencies (1977) and the Catholic Children's Society (1983). Accounts of the experience of being in care, sometimes with tragic consequences, are given by O'Neill (1981) and Quinn (1988).

Chapter 7   Preventing Child Abuse

Prevention and the effectiveness of preventative strategies are examined by Cohen (1983). The benefits and problems of teaching good parenting is discussed in Reynolds (1978). Preventative strategies based on the Kidscape project are detailed in Elliot (1986). Home-start is the subject of a comprehensive study by van der Eyken (1982).

Chapter 8   The Effects of Abuse – the Later Years

The key book aimed at helping adults who were abused as children is Gil (1984). This book also provides guidance to the siblings and spouses of abuse victims. It will, moreover, give workers insights into the problems encountered by colleagues and clients who have lived through an abusive childhood. For adult survivors interested in help through self-analysis, writing and poetry the *Journal of the Institute of Self-Analysis* may be useful. There are a large number of articles on group work with women sexually mistreated when young but an article by Bruckner and Johnson (1987) describes group work with men who were child sexual abuse victims.

Inquiry Reports

Published reports into the death or ill-treatment of a child or children are referred to by the children's name. Here they are listed in alphabetical order. The exception is the inquiry report into child abuse in Cleveland which is listed under 'Cleveland'.

Auckland (1975) *Report of the committee of inquiry into the provision of services to the family of J. G. Auckland,* London, HMSO.

Bagnall (1973) *Report of working party of social services committee inquiry into circumstances surrounding the death of Graham Bagnall and the role of the county social services,* Salop County Council.

Bagnall (1973) *Report of a committee of the hospital management committee into the circumstances leading up to the death of Graham Bagnall insofar as the hospital authority were concerned,* Shrewsbury Group Hospital Management Committee.

Beckford (1985) *A Child in Trust: the Report of the panel of inquiry into the circumstances surrounding the death of Jasmine Beckford,* London Borough of Brent.

Brewer (1977) *Report of the review panel appointed by Somerset Area Review Committee to consider the case of Wayne Brewer,* Somerset Area Review Committee.

Brown (1978) *Paul and L. Brown. Report of an inquiry held at Wallasey,* Wirral Borough Council and Wirral Area Health Authority.

Brown (1979) *An inquiry into an inquiry,* Birmingham, BASW.

Brown (1980) *The report of the committee of inquiry into the case of Paul Stephen Brown,* DHSS, Cmd 8107, London, HMSO.

Caesar (1982) *Report . . . on the involvement of the Social Services Department in the events preceding the Death of Jason Caesar,* Cambridge County Council.

Carlile (1987) *A Child in Mind: Protection of Children in a Responsible Society. The Report of the Commission of inquiry into the circumstances surrounding the death of Kimberley Carlile,* London Borough of Greenwich and Greenwich Health Authority.

Carthy (1985) *Report of the standing inquiry panel into the case of Reuben Carthy,* Nottinghamshire County Council.

127

Chapman (1979) *Lester Chapman inquiry report*, Berkshire County Council.

Clark (1975) *Report of the committee of inquiry into the considerations given and steps taken towards securing the welfare of Richard Clark by Perth Town and other bodies of persons concerned*, Scottish Education Department, Social Work Services Group, HMSO.

Clarke (1979) *The report of the committee of inquiry into the actions of the authorities and agencies relating to Darryn James Clarke*, DHSS, Cmnd 7730, London, HMSO.

Cleveland (1988) *Report of the Inquiry into Child Abuse in Cleveland 1987*, Cm 412, London, HMSO.

Colwell (1974) *Report of the Committee of enquiry into the care and supervision provided in relation to Maria Colwell*, London, HMSO.

Colwell (1975) *Children at Risk: A study into the problems revealed by the report of the inquiry into the case of Maria Colwell*, Lewes, East Sussex County Council.

Colwell (1976) *Children at Risk: Joint report of the County Secretary and Director of Social Services*, Lewes, East Sussex County Council.

Gates (1982) *Report of the panel of inquiry into the death of Lucy Gates, Vol. 1: Chairman's Report, Vol. 2: Report of other panel members*, London Borough of Bexley and Bexley Health Authority.

Godfrey (1975) *Report of the joint committee of enquiry into non-accidental injury to children with particular reference to Lisa Godfrey*, Lambeth, Southwark and Lewisham Health Authority (Teaching), Inner London Probation and After-Care Committee, London Borough of Lambeth.

'H' Family (1977) *the H. family: report of an investigation by the Director of Social Services and the Deputy Town Clerk*, Surrey County Council.

Haddon (1980) *Report of the Director of Social Services to the Social Services Committee, Clare Haddon born 9.12.78*, City of Birmingham Social Services Department.

Henry (1987) *Whose Child? The Report of the Panel Appointed to Inquire into the Death of Tyra Henry*, London Borough of Lambeth.

Howlett, (1976) *Joint enquiry arising from the death of Neil. Howlett*, City of Birmingham District Council and Birmingham Area Health Authority.

Koseda (1986) *Report of the review panel . . . into the death of Heidi Koseda*, London Borough of Hillingdon.

Mehmedagi (1981) *Maria Mehmedagi. Report of an independent inquiry*, London Borough of Southwark, Lambeth, Southwark and Lewisham Area Health Authority (Teaching), Inner London Probation and After-Care Service.

Menhenniott (1978) *Report of the Social Work Service of the DHSS into certain aspects of the management of the Case of Stephen Menheniott*, DHSS, London, HMSO.

Meurs (1975) *Report of the review body appointed to enquire into the case of Stephen Meurs*, Norfolk County Council.

Naseby (1973) *Report of the committee of enquiry set up to enquire into the circumstances surrounding the admission, treatment and discharge of baby David Lee Naseby, deceased at Burton-on-Trent General Hospital from February to May 1973*, Staffordshire Area Health Authority.

O'Neill (1945) *Report by Sir Walter Moncktom on the circumstances which led to the boarding out of Dennis and Terence O'Neill at Bank Farm, Miserley and the steps taken to supervise their welfare*, Cmnd 6636, London, HMSO.

Page (1981) *Malcolm Page. Report of a panel appointed by the Essex Area Review Committee*, Essex County Council and Essex Area Health Authority.

Peacock (1978) *Report of the committee of enquiry concerning Simon Peacock*, Cambridgeshire County Council, Suffolk County Council, Cambridgeshire AHA (Teaching), Suffolk AHA.

Piazzani (1974) *Report of the joint committee set up to consider co-ordination of services concerned with non-accidental injury to children*, Essex Area Health Authority and Essex County Council.

Pinder/Frankland (1981) *Child abuse enquiry sub-committee report concerning Christopher Pinder/Daniel Frankland (born 19.12.79, died 8.7.80)*. Bradford Area Review Committee.

Spencer (1978) *Karen Spencer*, Derbyshire County Council.

Taylor (1980) *Carly Taylor: report of an independent inquiry*, Leicestershire County Council and Leicestershire Area Health Authority (Teaching).

Woodcock (1984) *Report on the death of Shirley Woodcock*, London Borough of Hammersmith and Fulham.

This list was compiled with the assistance of Christine Smakowska (Librarian, NSPCC) and David N. Jones (General Secretary, BASW).

Bibliography

Adamson, J. and Warren, C. (1983) *Welcome to St Gabriel's Family Centre*, London, The Children's Society.

Angelou, M. (1984) *I Know Why the Cage Bird Sings*, London, Virago.

Association of British Adoption and Fostering Agencies (1977) *Working with Children who are Joining New Families*, London, ABAFA.

Bahn, C. (1980) 'Hostage takers, the taken and the context: discussion, *Annals of the New York Academy of Sciences*, No. 347, pp. 129–36.

Beezley Mrazek, P. and Mrazek, D. A. (1981) 'The Effects of Child Sexual Abuse: Methodological Considerations', in Beezley Mrazek, P. and Kempe, C. H. (eds), *Sexually Abused Children and their Families*, Oxford, Pergamon.

Bettleheim, B. (1979) *Surviving and Other Essays*, London, Thames & Hudson.

Bion, W. R. (1961) *Experiences in Groups and Other Papers*, London, Tavistock.

Blakey, C., Collinge, M. and Jones, D. N. (1986) 'The One-way Screen', *Community Care* 25 September 1986 pp. 16–17.

Bloch, D. (1979) *So the Witch Won't Eat Me, Fantasy and the Child's Fear of Infanticide*, London, Burnett Books.

Bolton, F. G. Jr. (1983) *When Bonding Fails: Clinical Assessment of High-Risk Families*, Beverly Hills, Sage Publications.

Bowlby, J. (1953) *Child Care and the Growth of Love*, Harmondsworth, Penguin.

Brim, O. G. Jr. (1965) *Education for Child Rearing*, New York, The Free Press.

Bruckner, D. F. and Johnson, P. E. (1987) 'Treatment of Adult Male Victims of Childhood Sexual Abuse', *Social Casework*, February 1987, pp. 81–7.

Button, L. (1974) *Developmental Group Work with Adolescents*, London, Hodder and Stoughton.

Cameronchild, J. (1987) 'An Autobiography of Violence', *Child Abuse and Neglect*, Vol. 2, pp. 139–49.

Carpenter, F. (1974) 'Mother's Face and the Newborn', *New Scientist*, 21 March, pp. 742–4.

Catholic Children's Society (1983) *Finding Out About Me*, London, CCS.

Chodoff, P. (1981) 'Survivors of the Nazi Holocaust' *Children Today*, Sept-Oct, pp. 2–5.

Cohen, A. H. (1983) 'The Prevention of Child Abuse: What do We Know About What Works?, in Leavitt, J. E. (ed.) *Child Abuse and Neglect: Research and Innovation*, The Hague, Martinus Nijhoff.

Cooper, C. (1985) "Good-enough", Borderline and "Bad-enough"

Parenting', in Adcock, M. and White, R. (eds), *Good-enough Parenting: a Framework for Assessment*, London, BAAF.

Cooper, D. M. and Ball, D. (1987) *Social Work and Child Abuse*, London, Macmillan.

Creighton, S. J. (1984) *Trends in Child Abuse 1977–1982*, London, NSPCC.

DHSS (1976) *Guide to Fostering Practice*, Report of the Working Party of Fostering Practice, London, HMSO.

DHSS (1988) *Present Day Practice in Infant Feeding: Third Report*, London, HMSO.

Dobson, C. and Payne, R. (1977) *The Carlos Complex: a Study in Terror*, London, Hodder & Stoughton.

Doyle, C. (1985) *The Imprisoned Child, Aspects of Rescuing the Severely Abused Child*, London, NSPCC Occasional Paper no. 3.

Doyle, C. (1986) 'Management Sensitivity in CSA Training, *Child Abuse Review*, Vol. 1, no. 4, pp. 8–9.

Doyle, C. (1987) 'Helping Child Victims of Sexual Abuse Through Play', *Practice*, Vol. 1, no. 1, pp. 27–38.

Elliot, M. (1986) *Keeping Safe, a Practical Guide to Talking with Children*, London, Bedford Square Press/NCVO.

Elton, A. (1988) 'Family Treatment – Treatment Methods and Techniques', in Bentovim, A., Elton, A., Hildebrand, J., Tranter, M. and Vizard, E. (eds), *Child Sexual Abuse within the Family: Assessment and Treatment*, London, Wright.

Erikson, E. H. (1965) *Childhood and Society*, 2nd edn, Harmondsworth, Penguin.

Fraiberg, S. (1952) 'Some Aspects of Casework with Children. 1. Understanding the Child Client', *Social Casework*, Vol. 33, no. 9, November 1952.

Furniss, T., Bigley-Miller, L. and Van Elburg, A. (1988) 'Goal-orientated Group Treatment for Sexually Abused Adolescent Girls', *British Journal of Psychiatry*, No 152, pp. 97–106.

Gelles, R. J. and Strauss, M. A. (1979) 'Family Experience and Public Support of the Death Penalty', in Gil, D. G. (ed.), *Child Abuse and Violence*, New York, AMS Press.

Gil, D. G. (1970) *Violence against Children, Physical Child Abuse in the United States*, Cambridge Mass., Harvard University Press.

Gil, E. M. (1984) *Out-growing the Pain: a Book for and about Adults Abused as Children*, San Francisco, C A, Launch.

Glaser, D. and Frosh, S. (1988) *Child Sexual Abuse*, London, Macmillan.

Green, A. H. (1978) 'Self-Destructive Behaviour in Battered Children', *American Journal of Psychiatry*, Vol. 135, no. 5, May 1978, pp. 579–82.

Griffiths, P. (1987) 'The Response to Childline', *Child Abuse Review*, Vol. 1, no. 7, pp. 22–4.

Grinde, V. T. (1987) 'Child Welfare in the Nordic Countries', *Child Abuse Review*, Vol. 1, no. 7, pp. 14–18.

Hildebrand, J. (1988) 'The Use of Groupwork in Treating Child Sexual Abuse', in Bentovim, A., Elton, A., Hildebrand, J., Tranter, M. and Vizard, E. (eds), *Child Sexual Abuse within the Family: Assessment and Treatment*, London, Wright.

Hindmann, J. (1983) *A Very Touching Book*, Durkes, Oregon, McClure-Hindmann.

Holgate, E. (ed.) (1972) *Communicating with Children: Collected Papers*, London, Longmann.

Jewett, C. (1984) *Helping Children Cope with Separation and Loss*, London, Batsford.

Jones, D. N., Pickett, J., Oates, M. R., and Barbor, P. (1987) *Understanding Child Abuse*, 2nd edn, London, Macmillan.

Jones, D. P. H. and McQuiston, M. (1985) *Interviewing the Sexually Abused Child*, Denver, The C. Henry Kempe National Centre for the Prevention and Treatment of Child Abuse and Neglect.

Kennell, J., Voos, D. and Klaus, M. (1976) 'Parent-infant bonding', in Helfer, R. E. and Kempe, C. H. (eds), *Child Abuse and Neglect*, Cambridge Mass., Ballinger.

Kezur, B. (1981) 'Play Therapy as a Mode of Treatment for Disturbed Children', in Martel, S. (ed.), *Direct Work with Children*, London, Bedford Square Press.

Konopka, G. (1972) *Social Group Work*, 2nd edn, Englewood Cliffs N. J., Prentice-Hall.

Leith, A. and Handforth, S. (1988) 'Groupwork with Sexually Abused Boys', *Practice*, Vol. 2, no. 2, pp. 166–75.

Leslie, G. R. (1982) *The Family in the Social Context*, 5th edn, New York, Oxford University Press.

Littner, N. (1956) *Some Traumatic Effects of Separation and Placement*, New York, Child Welfare League of America.

Lynch, M. A. and Roberts, J. (1982) *Consequences of Child Abuse*, London, Academic Press.

Macfarlane, A. (1977) *The Psychology of Childbirth*, London, Fontana/Open Books.

McFadden, E. J. (1980) 'Fostering and the Battered and Abused Child, *Children Today*, March-April 1980, pp. 13–15.

McKnight, R. (1972) 'Group work with Children', in Holgate, E. (ed.), *Communicating with Children: Collected Papers*, London, Longman.

Mayle, P. (1973) *Where Did I Come From?* Melbourne, Sun Books.

Mills, M. and Melhuish, E. (1974) 'Recognition of Mother's Voice in Early Infancy', *Nature*, No. 252, pp. 123–4.

Narducci, T. (1987) 'Breaking through the embarrassment barrier', *Community Care*, supplement, 25 June 1987 pp. iii-iv.

O'Neill, T. (1981) *A Place Called Hope. Caring for Children in Distress*, Oxford, Basil Blackwell.

Oppenheimer, R. (1985) 'Implications for Long Term Treatment', conference seminar summarised by Groves, F. in *Child Sexual Abuse – Report of the Inaugural Conference*, British Association for the Study and Prevention of Child Abuse and Neglect, Midlands Branch.

Parker, T. (1969) *The Twisting Lane, Some Sex Offenders*, London, Panther.

Parton, N. (1985) *The Politics of Child Abuse*, London, Macmillan.

Pelton, L. H. (ed.) (1981) *The Social Context of Child Abuse*, New York, Human Science Press.

Peters, J. (1966) *Growing-up World, Children in Families*, London, Longmans, p. 74.

Pizzey, E. (1974) *Scream Quietly or the Neighbours will Hear*, Harmondsworth, Penguin.

Quinn, P. (1988) *Cry Out!* Eastbourne, Kingsway.

Reidy, T. J. (1977) 'The Aggressive Characteristics of Abused and Neglected Children', *Journal of Clinical Psychology*, Vol. 33, no. 4, Oct. 1977, pp. 1140–45.

Reynolds, C. (1978) 'Can Good Parenting Be Taught', in Franklin, A. W. *Child Abuse: Prediction, Prevention and Follow-up*, Edinburgh, Churchill Livingstone.

Sebold, J. (1987) 'Indicators of Child Sexual Abuse in Males', *Social Casework*, February 1987, pp. 75–80.

Seligman, M. E. P. (1975) *Helplessness. On Depression, Development and Death*, San Francisco, W. H. Freeman.

Skinner, B. F. (1953) *Science and Human Behaviour*, London, Macmillan.

Skinner, S. and Kimmel, E. (1984) *The Anti-Colouring Book*, London, Scholastic Books.

Solzhenitsyn, A. (1974) *The Gulag Archipelago 1918–56*, Collins/Fontana.

Spring, J. (1987) *Cry Hard and Swim: the Story of an Incest Survivor*, London, Virago.

Stern, C. (1987) 'The Recognition of Child Abuse', in Maher, P. (ed.), *Child Abuse the Educational Practice*, Oxford, Blackwell.

Strenz, T. (1980) 'The Stockholm Syndrome. Law Enforcement, Policy and Ego Defenses of the Hostage, *Annals of the New York Academy of Sciences*, No. 347, pp. 137–50.

Summit, R. C. (1983) 'The Child Sexual Abuse Accomodation Syndrome', *Child Abuse and Neglect*, Vol. 7, pp. 177–93.

Symonds, M. (1980) 'Victim Responses to Terror', *Annals of the New York Academy of Sciences*, No. 347, pp. 129–36.

Thoburn, J. (1988) *Child Placement: Principles and Practice*, Wildwood House.

Thorndike, E. L. (1913) *The Psychology of Learning*, Teachers College Press.

Timberlake, E. M. (1979) 'Aggression and Depression among Abused and Non-abused Children in Foster Care', *Children and Youth Services Review*, No. 1. pp. 279–91.

van der Eyken, W. (1982) *Home-Start, a Four-year Evaluation*, Leicester, Home-Start Consultancy.

Vizard, E. (1987) 'Self Esteem and Personal Safety', in *ACPP Newsletter*, Vol. 9, no. 2, pp.16–22.

Vizard, E. and Tranter, M. (1988) 'Helping Children to Describe Experiences of Child Sexual Abuse – A Guide to Practice', in Bentovim, A., Elton, A., Hildebrand, J., Tranter, M. and Vizard, E. (eds), *Child Sexual Abuse Within the Family: Assessment and Treatment*, London, Wright.

Wratten, R. (1985) 'Predicting a Family's Response to Treatment', in Adcock, M. and White, R. (eds), *Good-enough Parenting: a Framework for Assessment*, London, BAAF.

Wolfe, D. A. (1987) *Child Abuse: Implications for Child Development and Psychopathology*, London, Sage Publications.

Wyre, R. (1986) *Men, Women and Rape*, Oxford, Perry.

Yule, V. C. (1985) 'Why are Parents Tough on Children?' *New Society* 27 September 1985, pp. 444–6.

Zigler, E. (1979) 'Controlling Child Abuse in America: An Effort Doomed to Failure', in Gil, D. G. (ed.), *Child Abuse and Violence*, New York, AMS Press.

Index

134